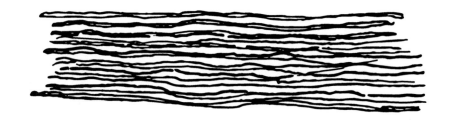

PAPER DOLL ORGY

Drawings by Ted McCagg

Published by The Nervous Breakdown Books
Los Angeles, California
www.thenervousbreakdown.com

First Edition, December 2010
Copyright © 2010 Ted McCagg

Book Design: Charlotte Howard, CKH Design

Design, programming and distribution for all digital editions:
Joseph Matheny of Hukilau.us

The views expressed in this book are those of the author
and do not necessarily reflect those of the publisher.

The text face is set in Baskerville, because we are Sherlock Holmes.

ISBN 978-0-9828598-2-7

Printed in the United States of America

To Kate, for providing the laughs, no matter how forced.

To Viv, who will almost certainly be embarrassed about my work in the future.

And to McCann Erickson, without whose brain-numbing, soul-killing freelance job I would have never found the need to do something creative everyday, and thus, started to produce these drawings.

INTRODUCTION

The First Drawing I remember doing was of an elephant perched on the peak of a dangerously pointy mountain. It looked sort of like this:

I don't remember actually drawing it. I don't remember coming up with the backstory for why an elephant was on the mountain in the first place. Was he on the run from poachers? As a baby, was he snatched in the talons of a large eagle and dropped on this treacherous peak, where he has grown old eating curious mountain goats and scatterbrained small birds? Was this a sex thing?

What I do remember is being proud of it. It was something that came from my brain, unprompted by a teacher's assignment or after-school art class. The longer it stayed on the fridge (and it stayed there for a surprisingly long time), the prouder I became.

When I draw something today, it's for the same reason. To see what the fuck my brain will come up with. To see just what disparate bits of knowledge I can piece together in one infantile sketch. And while they all can't be elephants on mountaintops, I'm still proud of each drawing I do.

Except "Glory Hole." That one is just downright embarrassing.

Fuck Me Pumps

Dry Hump Me Pumps

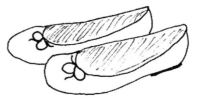

Spoon With Me
Fully Clothed Pumps

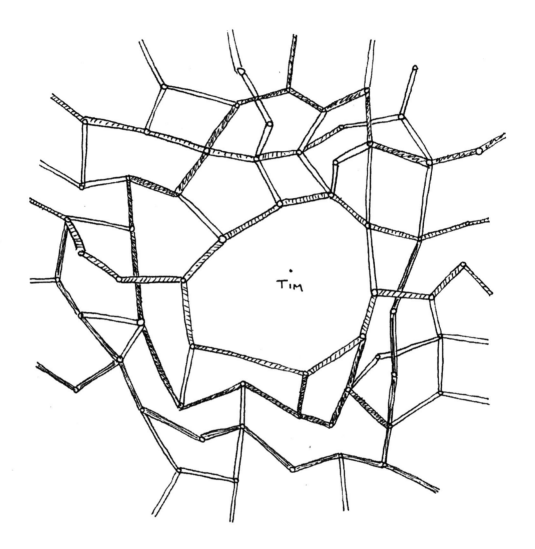

Tim

THE PARIS SUBWAY SYSTEM WAS DESIGNED AND
BUILT IN THE EARLY 1920s TO AVOID
A GUY NAMED TIM.

Slug Cop

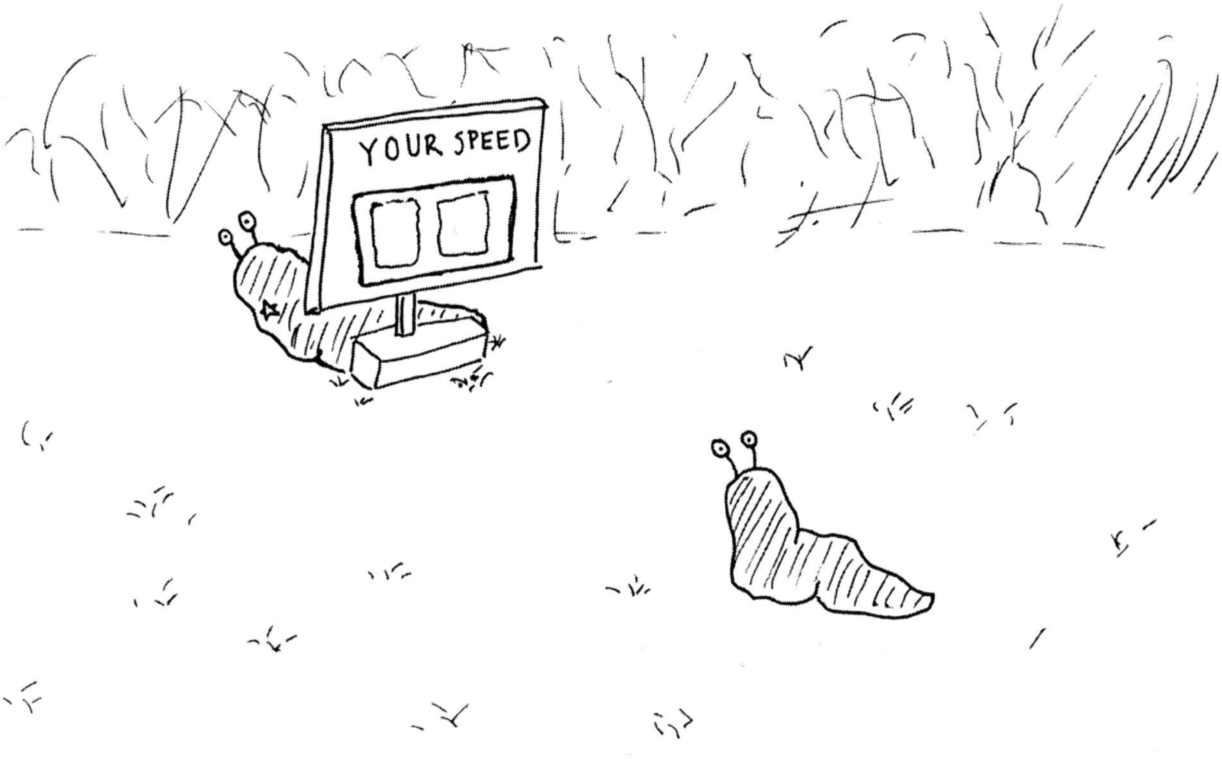
YOUR SPEED

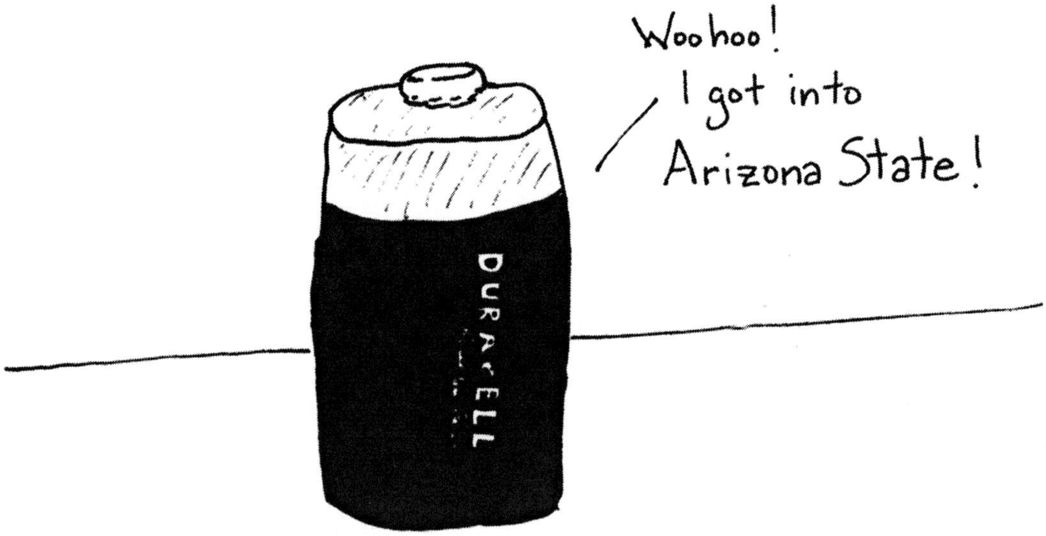
Woohoo!
I got into
Arizona State!
DURACELL

C BATTERY

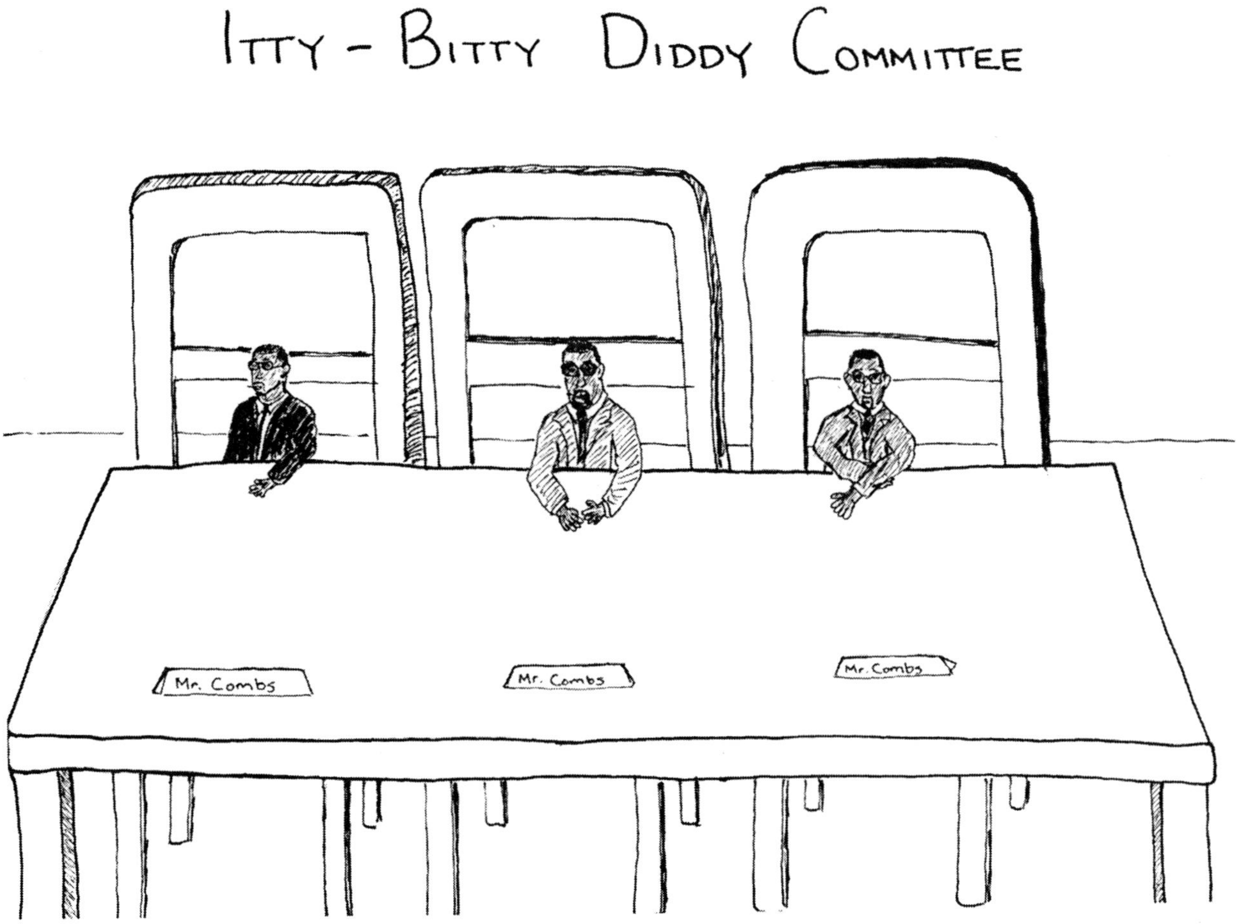
Itty - Bitty Diddy Committee
Mr. Combs
Mr. Combs
Mr. Combs

THE LAST KEGGER

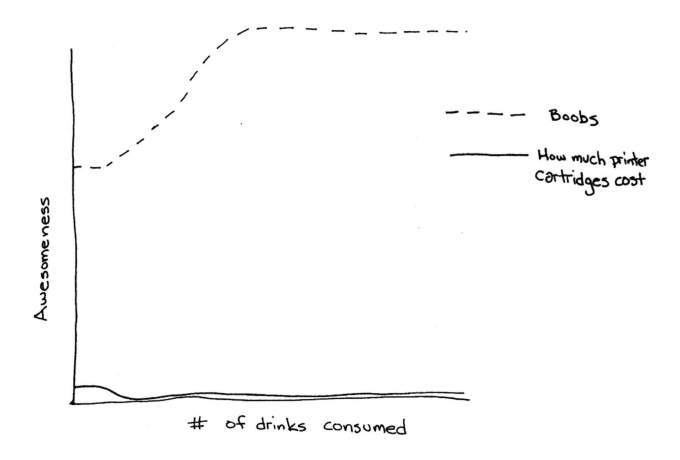

Boobs

How much printer cartridges cost

Awesomeness

# of drinks consumed

PAUL WAS BORN INSECURE.

Sorry about the episiotomy.

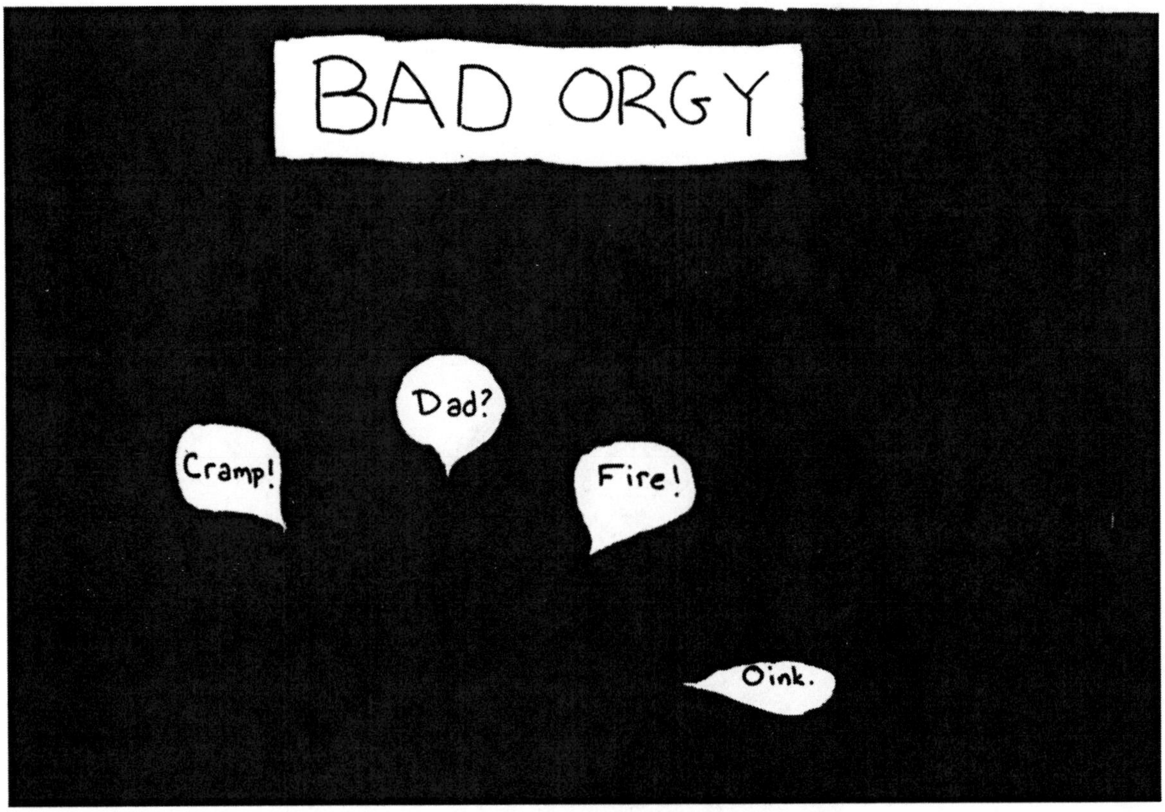
BAD ORGY
Cramp!
Dad?
Fire!
Oink.

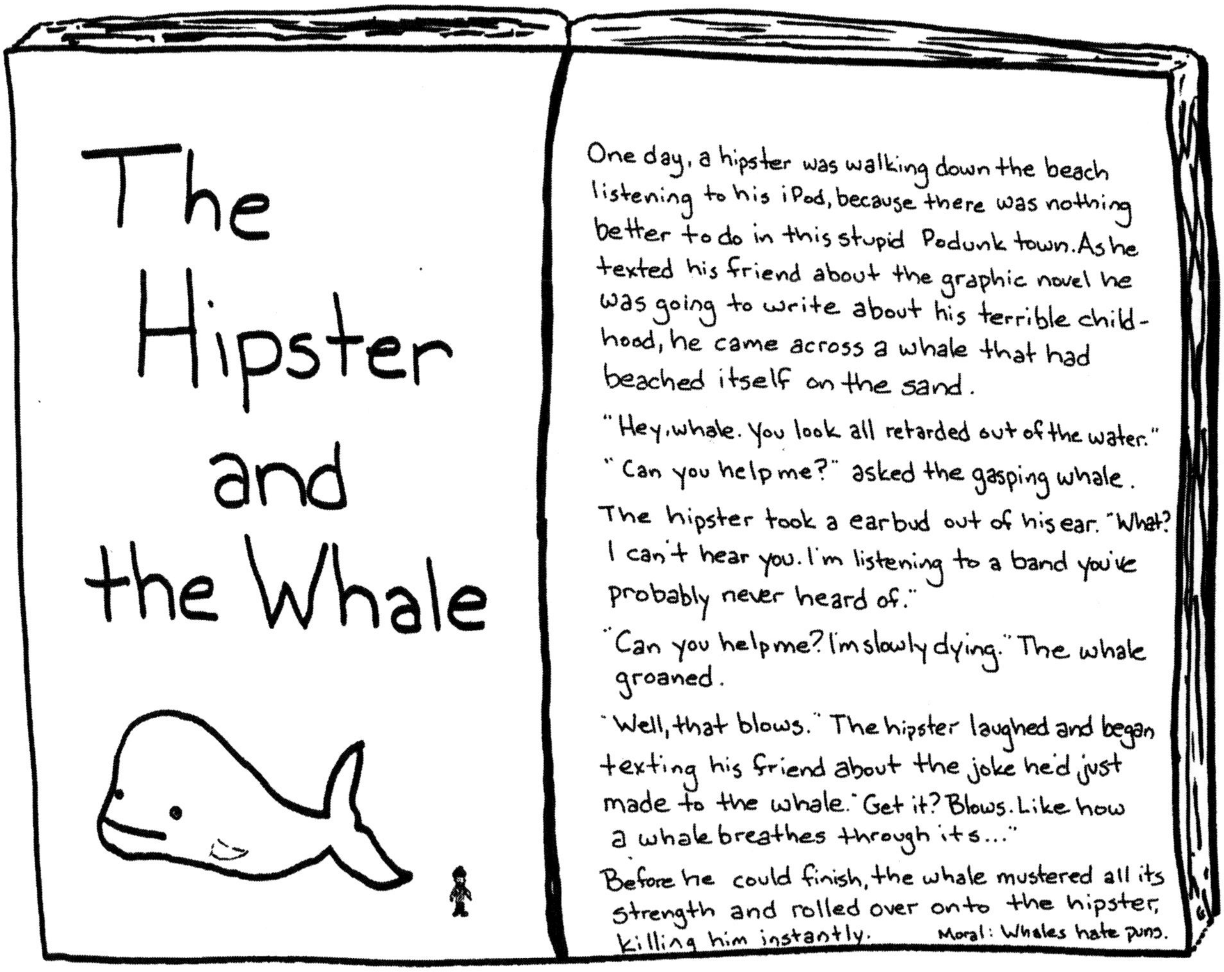
The Hipster and the Whale
One day, a hipster was walking down the beach listening to his iPod, because there was nothing better to do in this stupid Podunk town. As he texted his friend about the graphic novel he was going to write about his terrible childhood, he came across a whale that had beached itself on the sand.
"Hey, whale. You look all retarded out of the water."
"Can you help me?" asked the gasping whale.
The hipster took a earbud out of his ear. "What? I can't hear you. I'm listening to a band you've probably never heard of."
"Can you help me? I'm slowly dying." The whale groaned.
"Well, that blows." The hipster laughed and began texting his friend about the joke he'd just made to the whale. "Get it? Blows. Like how a whale breathes through its..."
Before he could finish, the whale mustered all its strength and rolled over onto the hipster, killing him instantly.
Moral: Whales hate puns.

BEACH SCENE WITH WILD THING

SAD HAIKU: LETTER

"It's not you, it's me,"
the note read. "I want to see
other people. — Mom."

— Daryll

KIDS SAY THE
DARNDEST THINGS!!

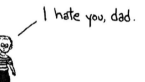 I hate you, dad.

BALL BEARING BEARING BALLS

IT WOULD BE HIS
MOST CHALLENGING CARICATURE EVER.

Oh my God, I feel like an asshole.

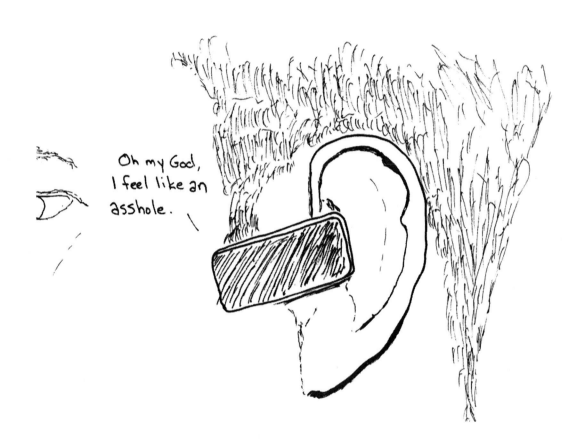

Bluetooth Headset Thoughts

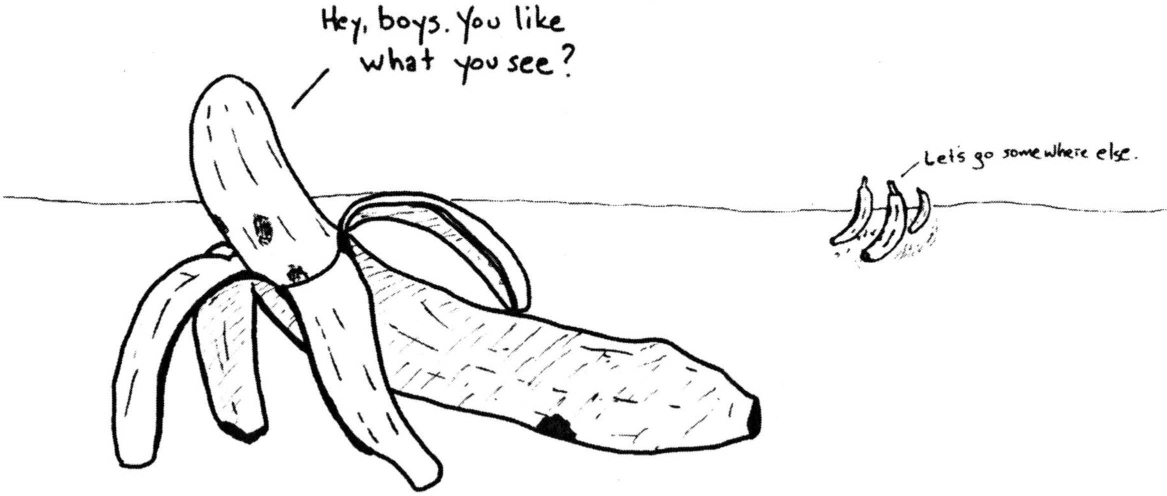
Hey, boys. You like what you see?
Let's go somewhere else.

COUGAR BANANA

INSPIRE GREATNESS*

* If that fails, provoke resentful one-upmanship.

Can you rub my foot for good luck? Sure, that makes sense. Can I sock you in the nuts and hope money comes out your mouth?

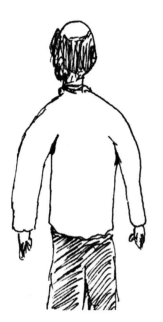

Bill The Belligerent Bunny Visits The OTB.

SAD HAIKU: WIND

Its been twenty years

Since I last touched a woman

The wind blows. Boner.

—Martin

CALIFORNIA, WITH KANGOL

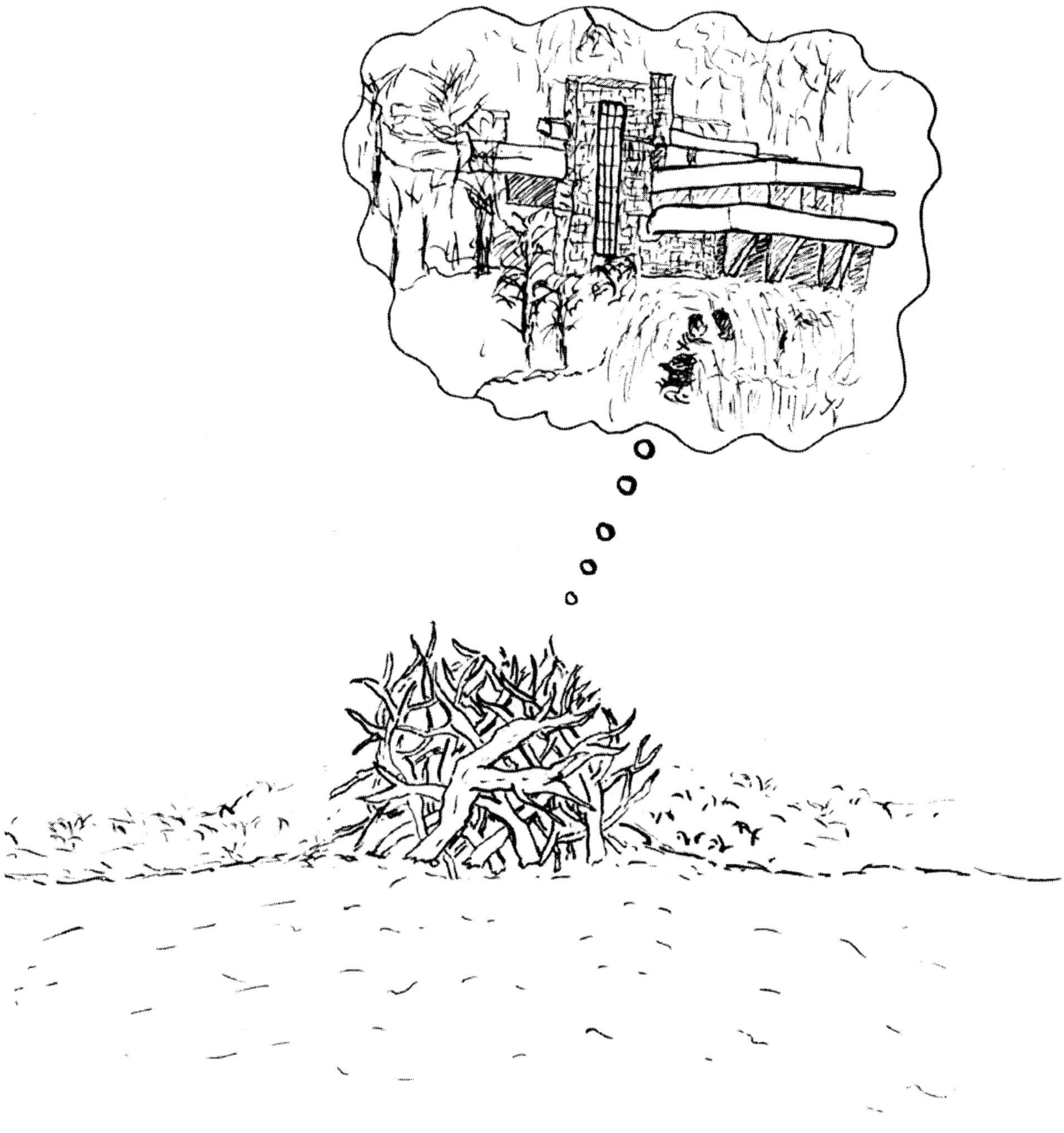

CHIP N' DALE'S CHIPPENDALES

COLORADO, UPSIDE DOWN

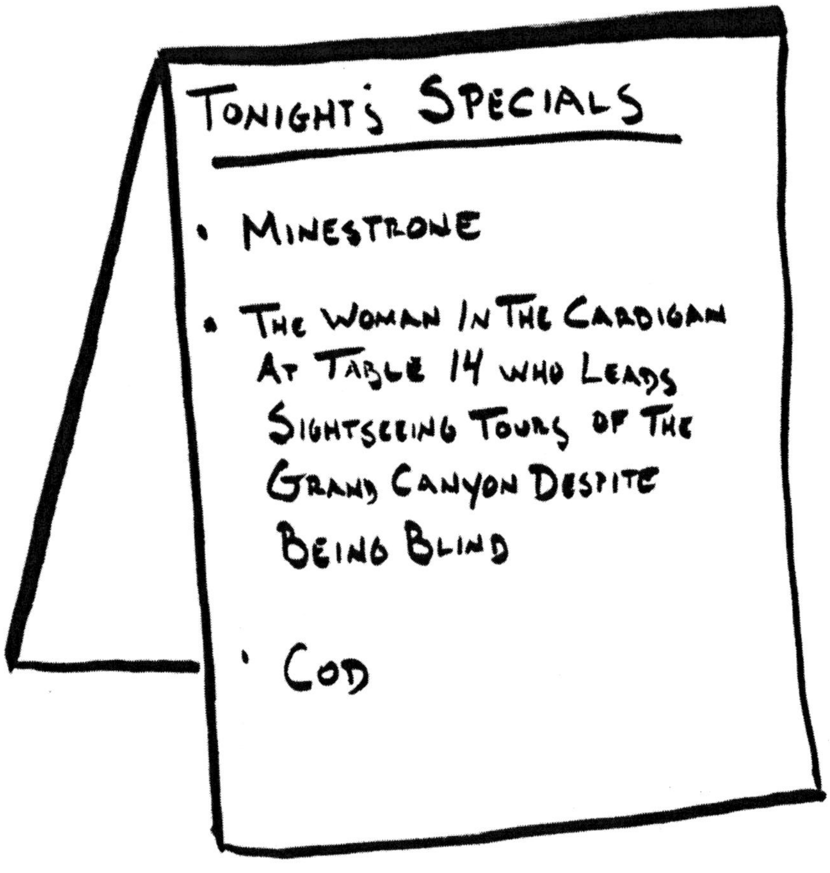
TONIGHT'S SPECIALS
• MINESTRONE
• THE WOMAN IN THE CARDIGAN AT TABLE 14 WHO LEADS SIGHTSEEING TOURS OF THE GRAND CANYON DESPITE BEING BLIND
• COD

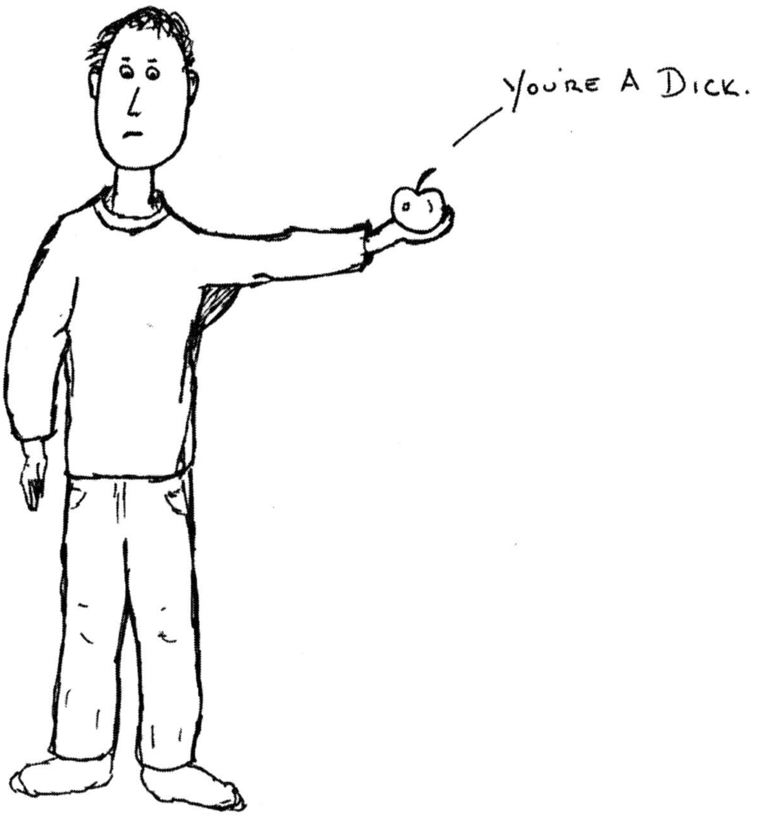
YOU'RE A DICK.

MY LEAST FAVORITE APPLE:
THE SOUR APPLE

When you assume,

Ich bin nicht
ein Esel.

You make an ass of Ume.

CONSERVATIVE

KIDZ BOP

6

Includes:
I Kissed A Girl
(and it was unnatural)

BERTIGO

NICK COLLECTED BIRDS DRAWN FROM A DISTANCE.

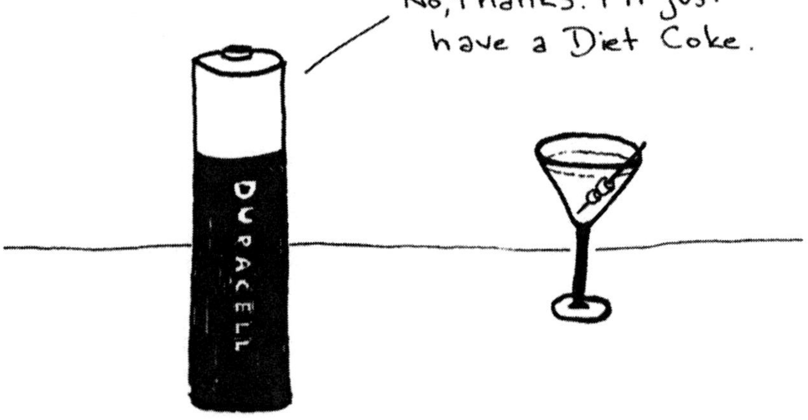
No, thanks. I'll just have a Diet Coke.
DURACELL

AA BATTERY

SAD HAIKU: SEATTLE HALLOWEEN

I am Lizard Boy!
Crazy, deadly, feared by all.
Trapped in a poncho.

- Billy

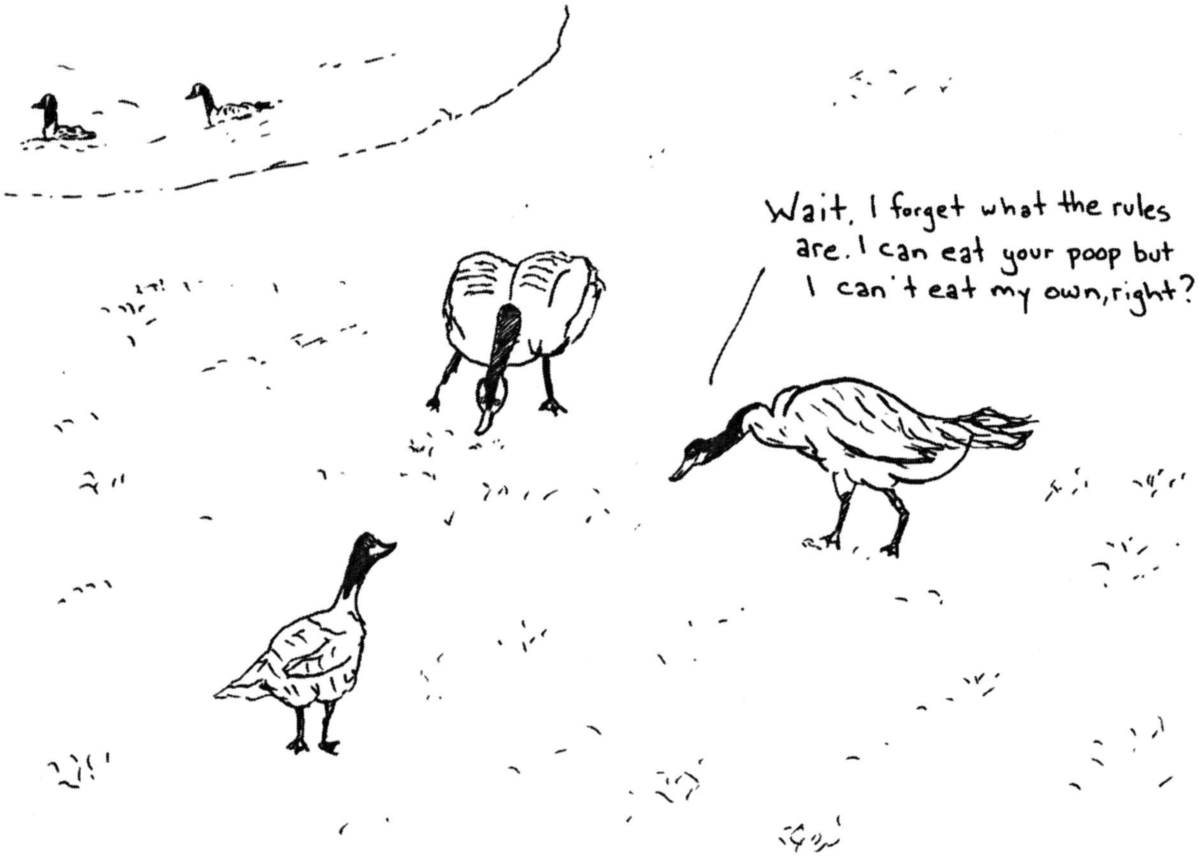
Wait, I forget what the rules are. I can eat your poop but I can't eat my own, right?

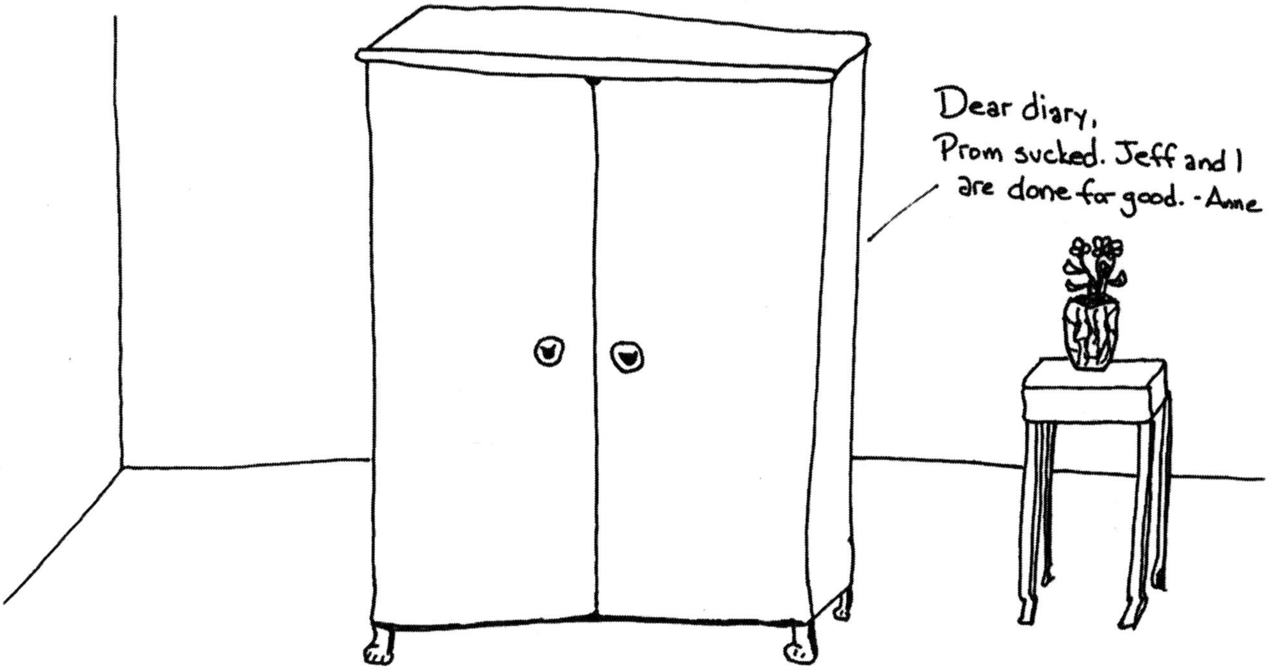
Dear diary,
Prom sucked. Jeff and I are done for good. -Anne

THE DIARY OF ANNE FRANK 2: SENIOR YEAR

Time Serving Options

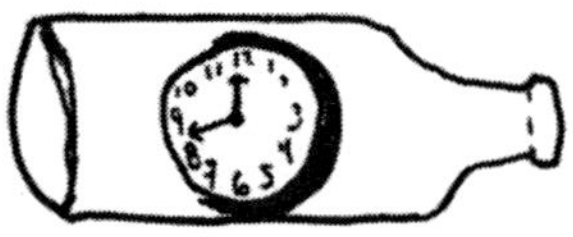

... in a bottle

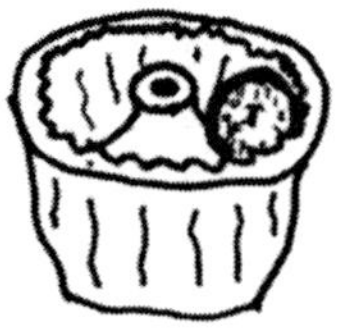

... in a bundt pan

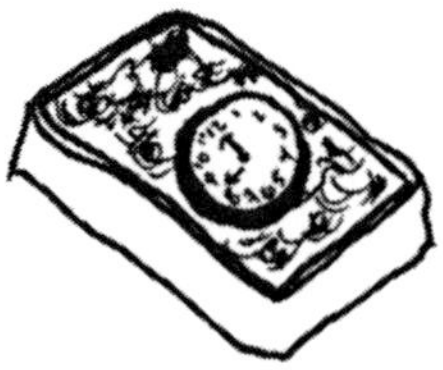

... au gratin

FORTUNATELY, HE HAD TAKEN "CONVERSATIONAL ZAPF DINGBATS" IN COLLEGE.

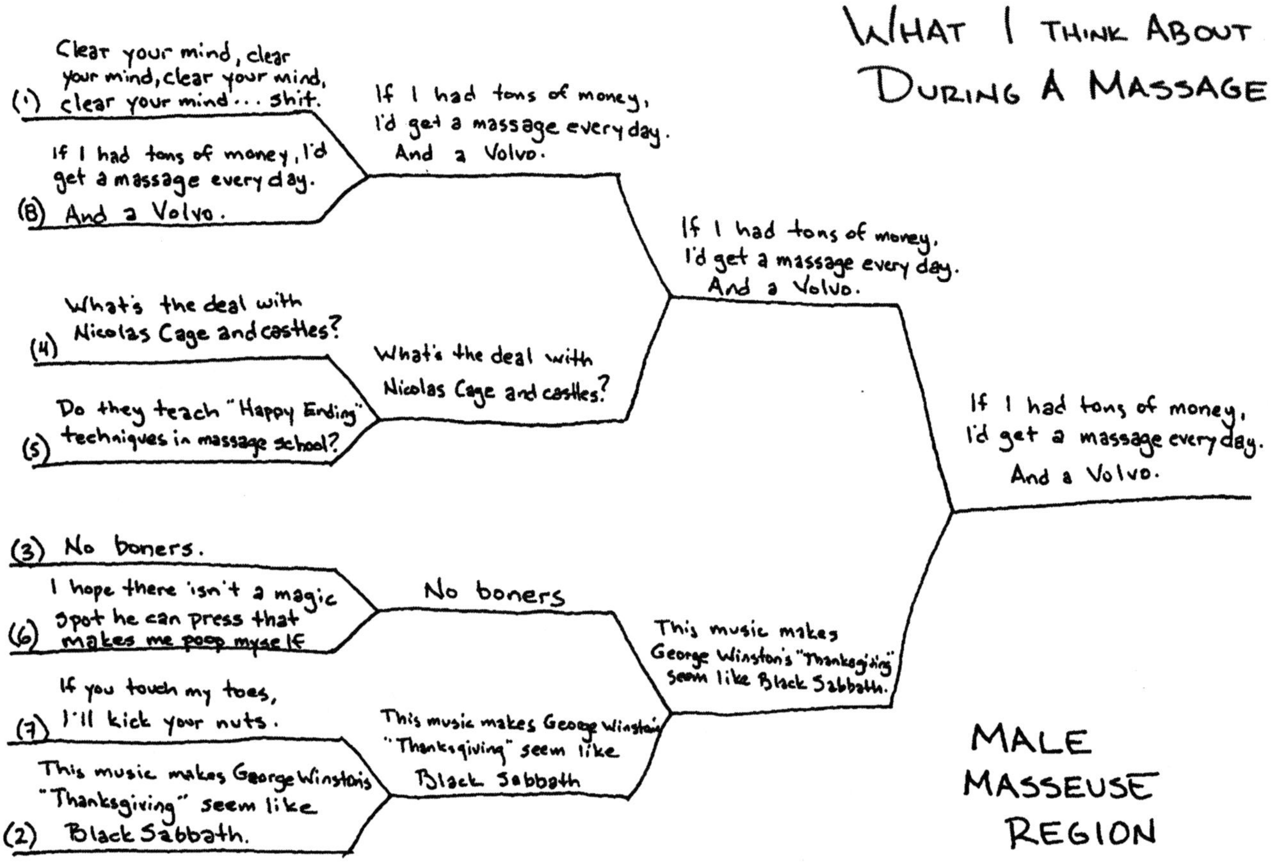

WHAT I THINK ABOUT DURING A MASSAGE
(1) Clear your mind, clear your mind, clear your mind, clear your mind... shit.
(8) If I had tons of money, I'd get a massage every day. And a Volvo.
If I had tons of money, I'd get a massage every day. And a Volvo.
(4) What's the deal with Nicolas Cage and castles?
(5) Do they teach "Happy Ending" techniques in massage school?
What's the deal with Nicolas Cage and castles?
If I had tons of money, I'd get a massage every day. And a Volvo.
(3) No boners.
(6) I hope there isn't a magic spot he can press that makes me poop myself
No boners
(7) If you touch my toes, I'll kick your nuts.
(2) This music makes George Winston's "Thanksgiving" seem like Black Sabbath.
This music makes George Winston's "Thanksgiving" seem like Black Sabbath
This music makes George Winston's "Thanksgiving" seem like Black Sabbath.
If I had tons of money, I'd get a massage every day. And a Volvo.
MALE MASSEUSE REGION

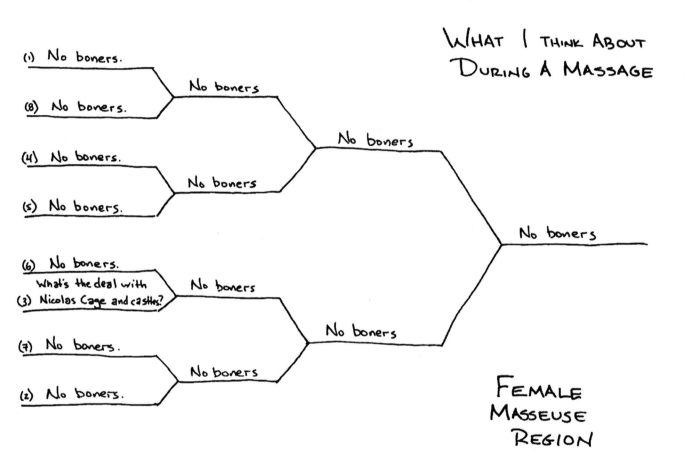

WHAT I THINK ABOUT DURING A MASSAGE
(1) No boners.
(8) No boners.
(4) No boners.
(5) No boners.
(6) No boners.
(3) What's the deal with Nicolas Cage and castles?
(7) No boners.
(2) No boners.
No boners
No boners
No boners
No boners
No boners
No boners
No boners
FEMALE MASSEUSE REGION

PLACES TO HIDE
here   here

A SMALL PIECE
here   here
here

OF CHOCOLATE.
here
here

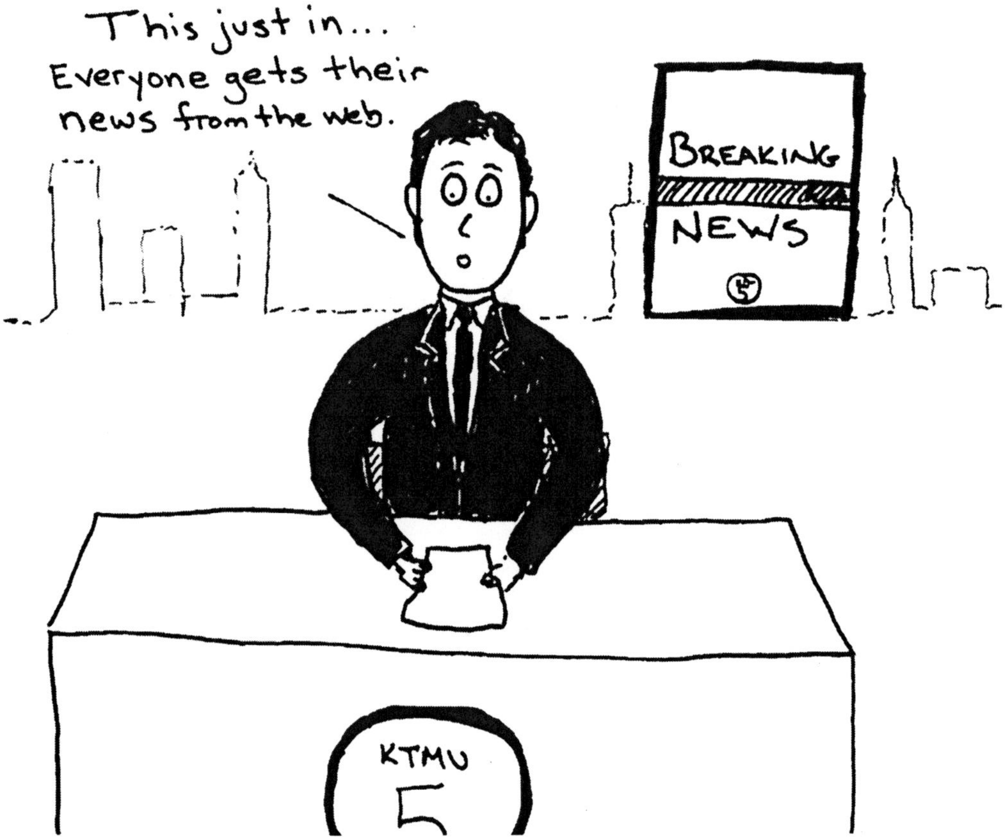
This just in... Everyone gets their news from the web.
BREAKING
NEWS
KTMU
5

I feel the need...
the need for speed!

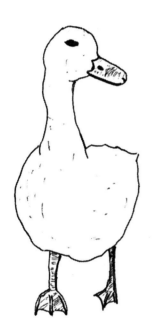

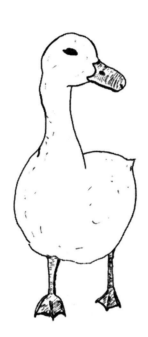

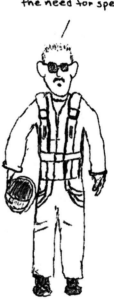

Duck Duck Goose

LEFT BRAIN VS RIGHT BRAIN

A HOT DOG IS A
TYPE OF FULLY-COOKED,
CURED, AND/OR SMOKED
SAUSAGE, USUALLY
PLACED HOT IN A SLICED
BUN OF THE SAME
LENGTH AS THE SAUSAGE.

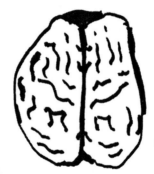

MADE FROM RAT'S NUTS
LOOKS LIKE A DUDE'S
DING DONG
DEE-LISH !!!

TOPIC: HOT DOGS

HE HAD THE NORTH DAKOTA DREAM AGAIN.

BILLY'S LAST FAMILY CIRCUS

Forbes

5,000,000,000

The Five Billion Wealthiest People
in the world

NUMBER	NAME, LOCATION	SOURCE OF WEALTH
3,572,911,001	Timmy Watkins, USA	Other Kid's Lunch Money
3,572,911,002	Manisha Junjee, India	Funeral Pyre Supplier / Children's Party Entertainer
3,572,911,003	Vlad Netson, Russia	Black Market Newman's Own Salad Dressing Sales
3,572,911,004	Syd Jamison, Australia	Paul Hogan Impersonator
3,572,911,005	Kyl Jörgenson, Sweden	Assorted Small Pelts
3,572,911,006	Mitch Myers, USA	Online "Go Fish" Tournaments
3,572,911,007	Sybil Jean, France	Snails
3,572,911,008	Yung Kim, Japan	Koncho Professional
3,572,911,009	Fran Donaldson, USA	Decoupage
3,572,911,010	Tsr Bnrft, Kenya	Prop Comic
3,572,911,011	Hing S. Kwan, Thailand	Police Lineup Decoy

ENCYCLOPEDIA BROWN AND THE CASE OF WHY
NOBODY CAME TO ENCYCLOPEDIA BROWN'S PARTY.

LESS STANS. MORE FREDS.

UK
RAI
NE

↑
MORE
RUSSIA

RUSSIA

KAZAKHFRED

GEORGIA

TURKEY

ARMENIA

A LONG COUNTRY NAME

CASPIAN SEA

UZBEKIFRED

KYRGYZFRED

TURKMENIFRED

TAJIKFRED

CHINA

SYRIA

IRAN

AFGHANIFRED

PAKIFRED

INDIA

IRAQ

GOLDEN GOSSIP GIRL

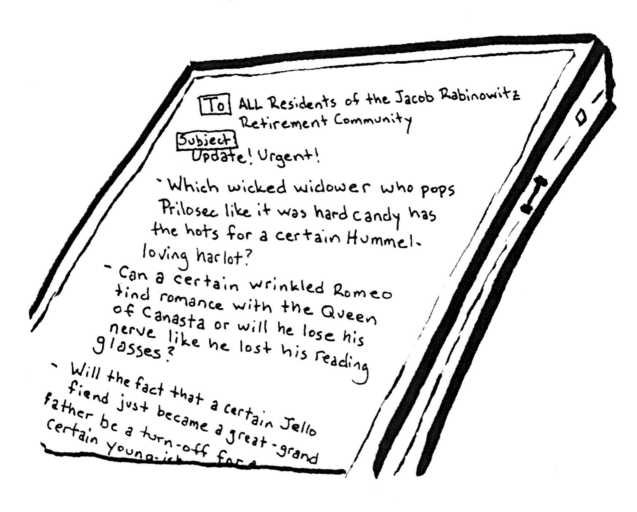

To ALL Residents of the Jacob Rabinowitz Retirement Community

Subject Update! Urgent!

- Which wicked widower who pops Prilosec like it was hard candy has the hots for a certain Hummel-loving harlot?

- Can a certain wrinkled Romeo find romance with the Queen of Canasta or will he lose his nerve like he lost his reading glasses?

- Will the fact that a certain Jello fiend just became a great-grand father be a turn-off for a certain young-ish

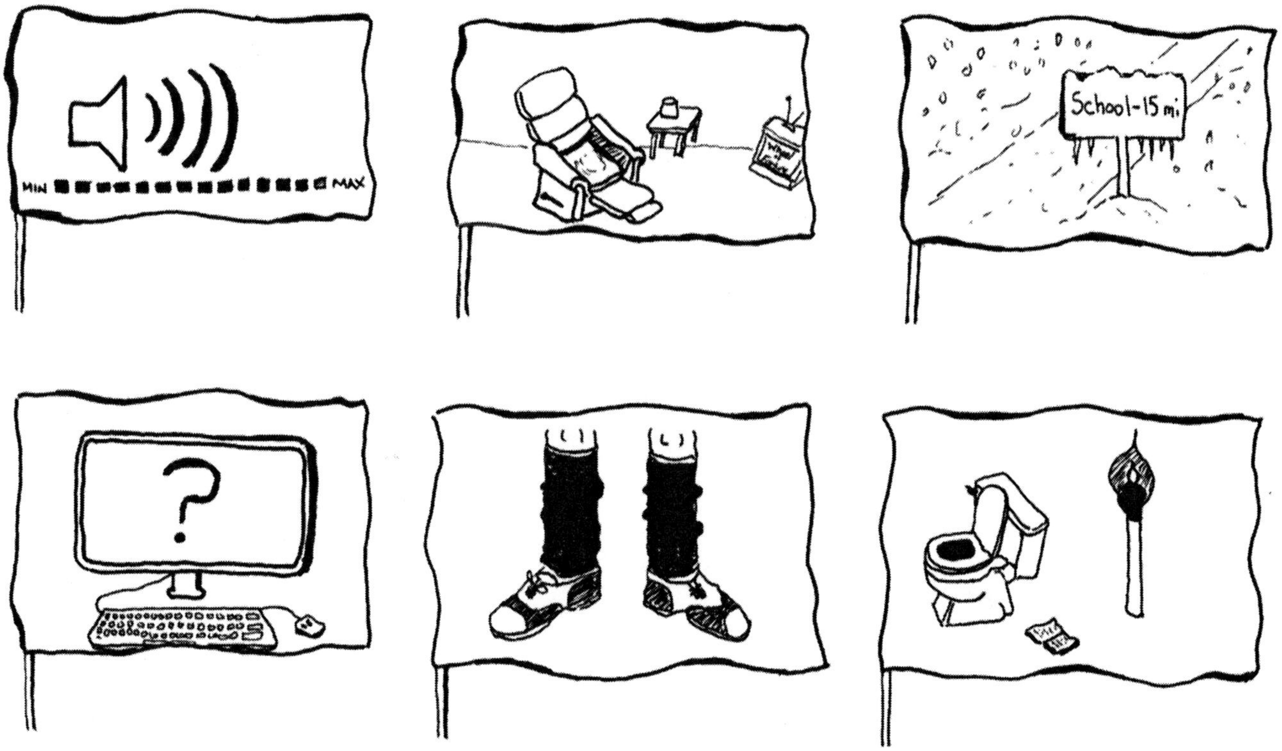
MIN
MAX
School-15 mi

FLAGS OF OUR FATHERS

This last pageant win

Puts me one step closer to

A life on the pole.

— Cindee

Sad Haiku: Lil' Miss Tampa

GLORY HOLE

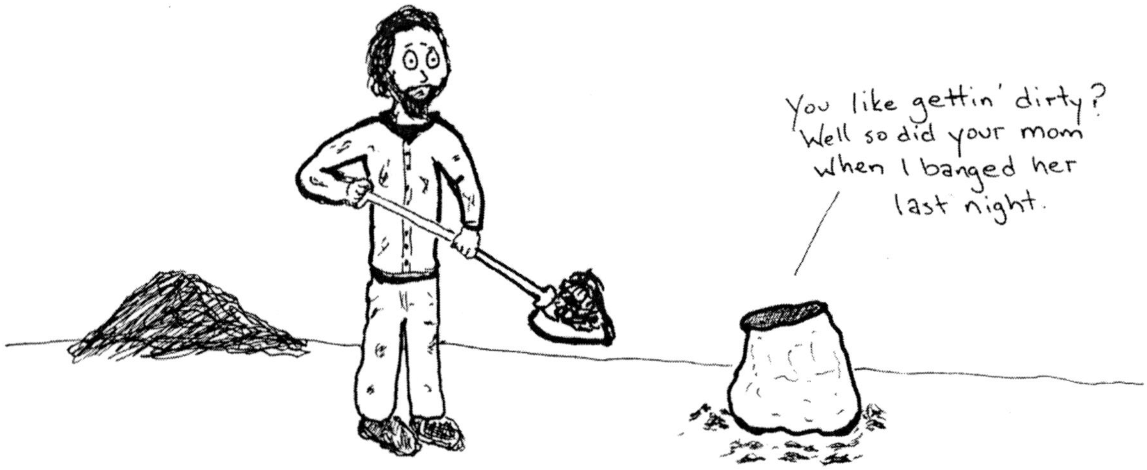
You like gettin' dirty? Well so did your mom when I banged her last night.

Unsuccessful Recurring Character: Dan The Dirtbag Dirt Bag

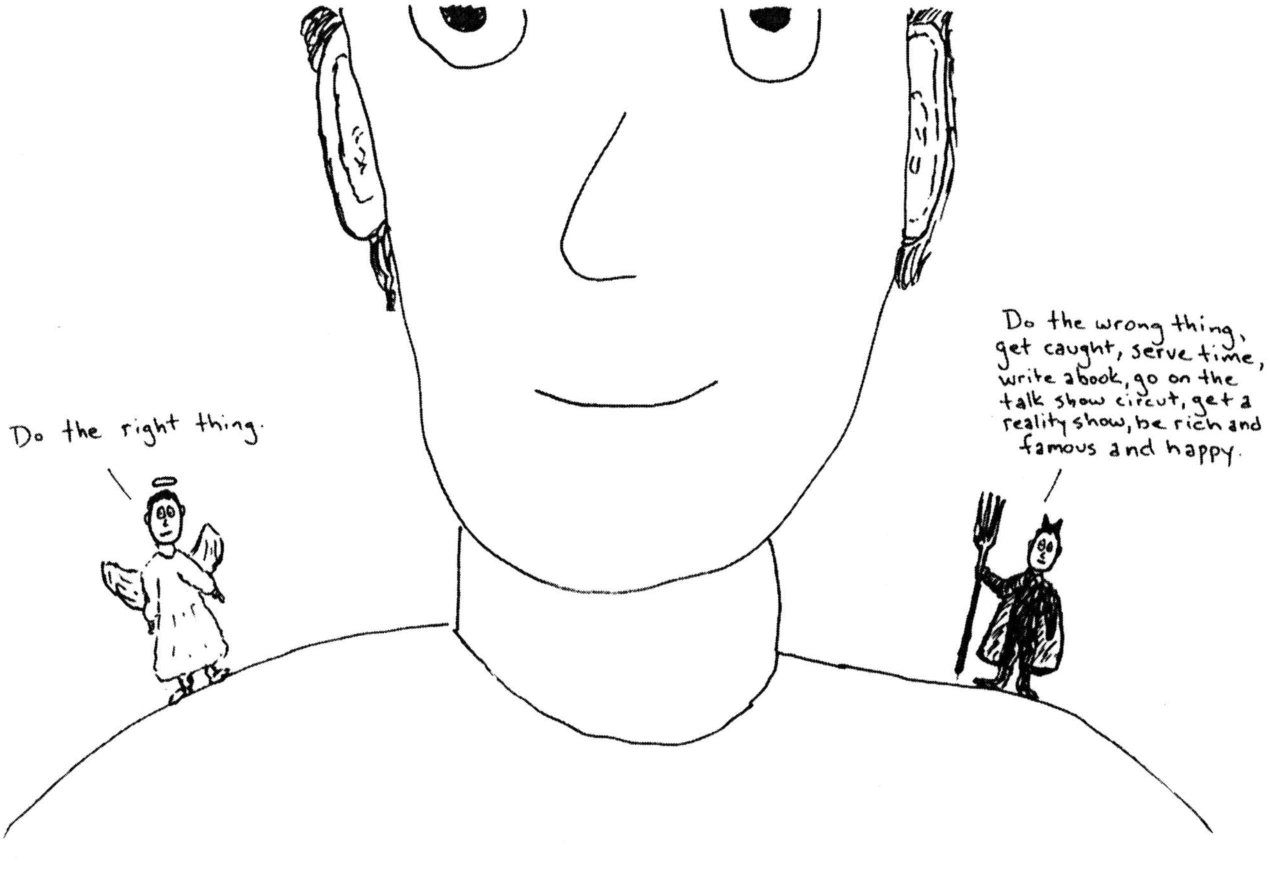
Do the right thing.
Do the wrong thing, get caught, serve time, write a book, go on the talk show circut, get a reality show, be rich and famous and happy.

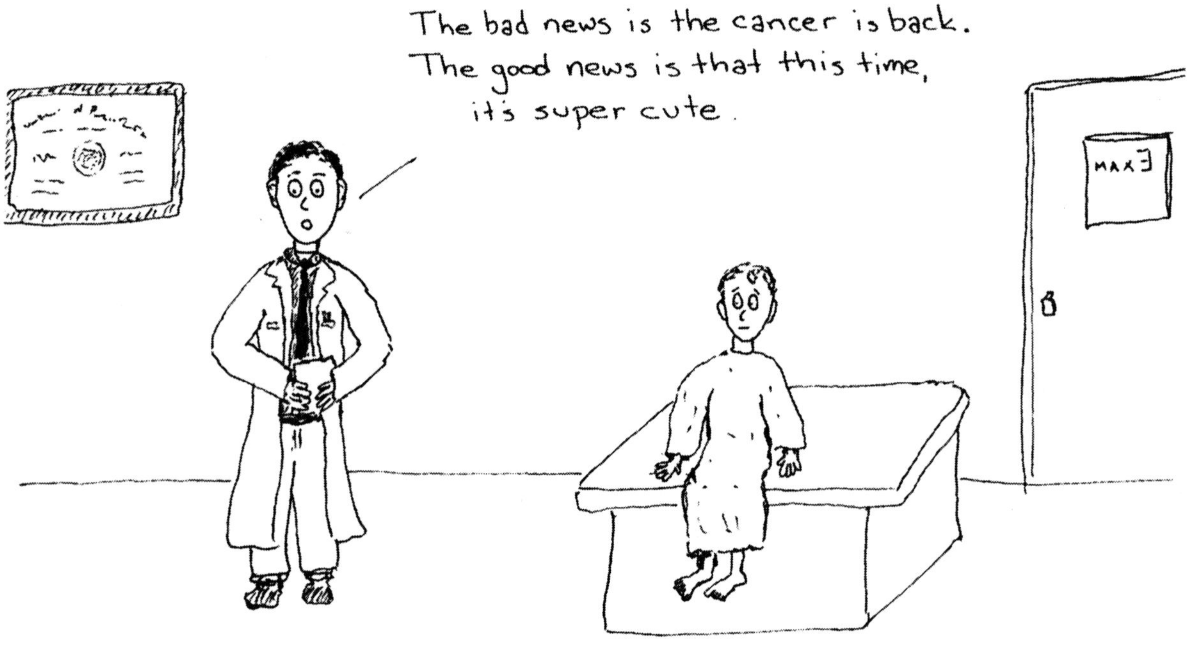
The bad news is the cancer is back. The good news is that this time, it's super cute.

A rare wild hand turkey sighting.

I went to my happy place
today, but when I got there,
I discovered that someone
had broken in and pooped
on the sheets.

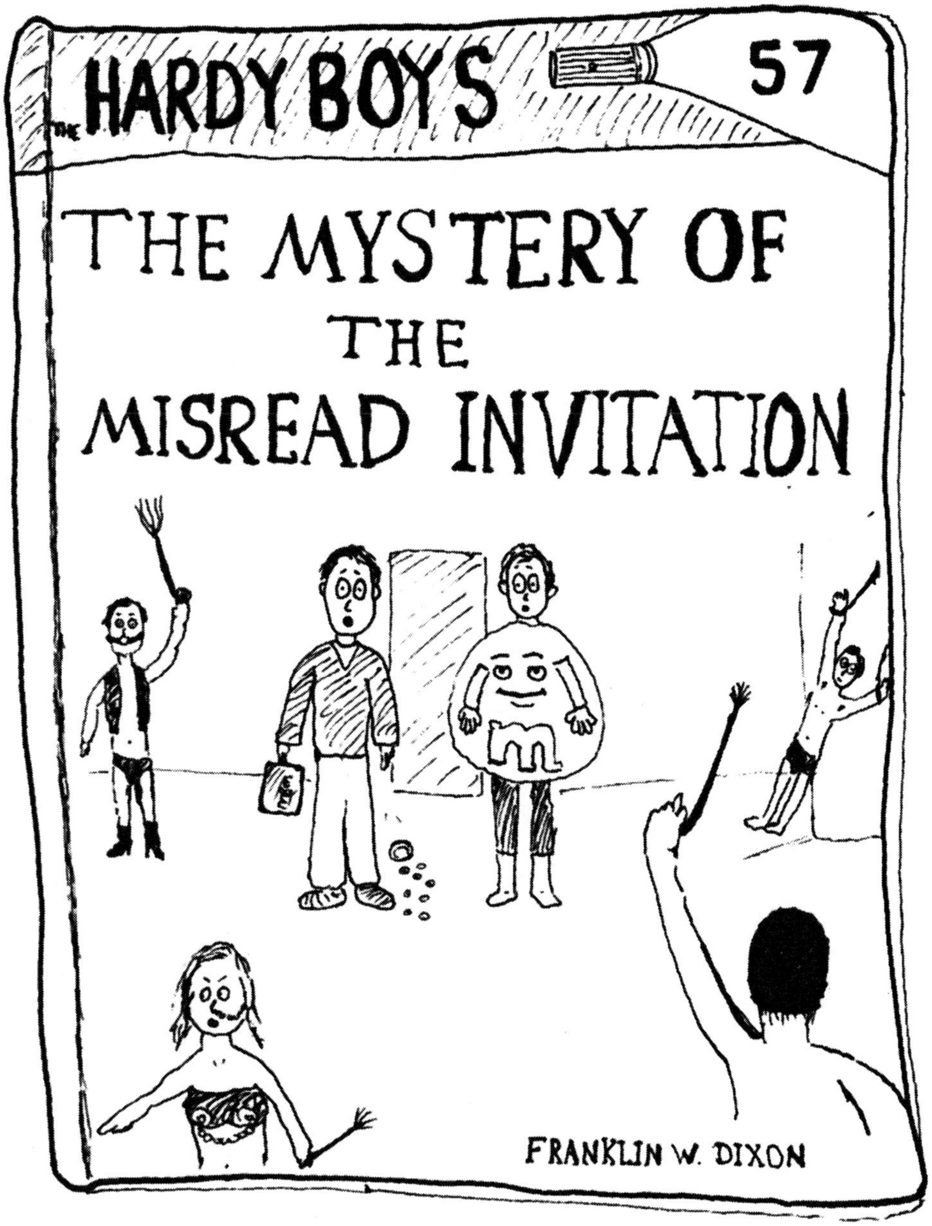
THE HARDY BOYS
57
THE MYSTERY OF
THE
MISREAD INVITATION
FRANKLIN W. DIXON

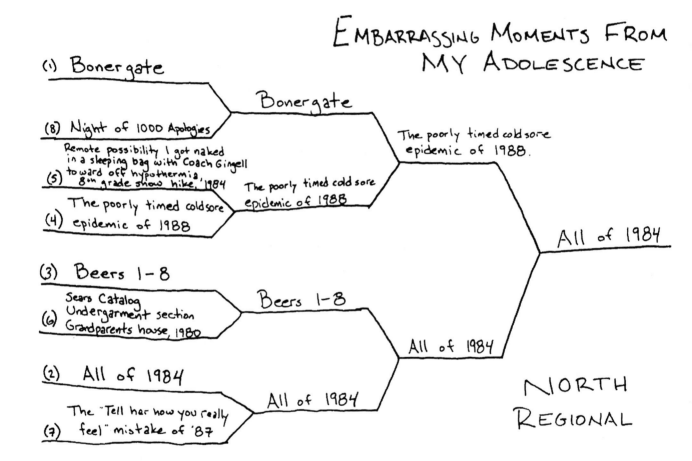

EMBARRASSING MOMENTS FROM MY ADOLESCENCE

(1) Bonergate

Bonergate

(8) Night of 1000 Apologies

Remote possibility I got naked
in a sleeping bag with Coach Gingell
(5) to ward off hypothermia,
8th grade snow hike, 1984

The poorly timed cold sore
epidemic of 1988

The poorly timed cold sore
epidemic of 1988.

The poorly timed cold sore
(4) epidemic of 1988

The poorly timed cold sore
epidemic of 1988

(3) Beers 1-8

Sears Catalog
Undergarment section
(6) Grandparents house, 1980

Beers 1-8

All of 1984

All of 1984

(2) All of 1984

All of 1984

The "Tell her how you really
(7) feel" mistake of '87

All of 1984

NORTH
REGIONAL

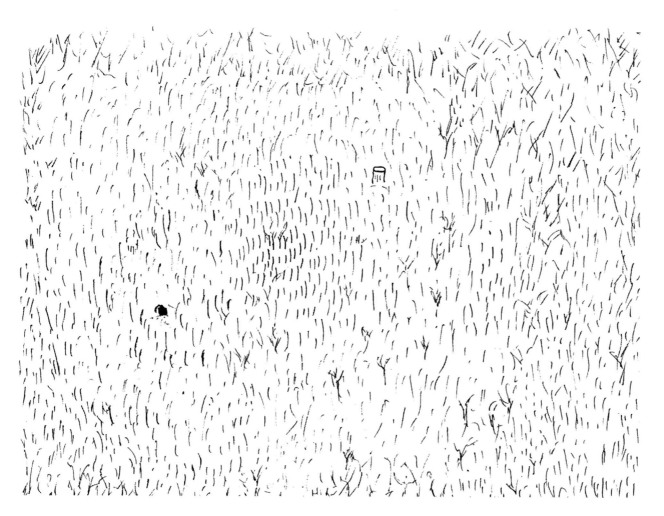

SHRINER CHASING CHEF THROUGH FIELD OF WHEAT

Hipster Porn

TILT SHIFT TANGO
TWO HOURS OF TINY, BLURRY ACTION
Etsy Orgy
Hand-crafted and hot!!
Spike Jonze Eats Gazpacho
It's gotta be cool. It's Spike Jonze!

THE LEGENDARY TRIPLE-BREASTED JACKET

THE HUNCHBACK OF PHILIP JOHNSON'S GLASS HOUSE.

Anal retentive people
must totally resent
being associated with
the word "anal."

TRIPLE LETTER SCORE
TRIPLE LETTER SCORE
DOUBLE LETTER SCORE
DOUBLE LETTER SCORE
U1
M3
DOUBLE LETTER SCORE
H4
DOUBLE LETTER SCORE
TRIPLE LETTER SCORE
TRIPLE LETTER SCORE

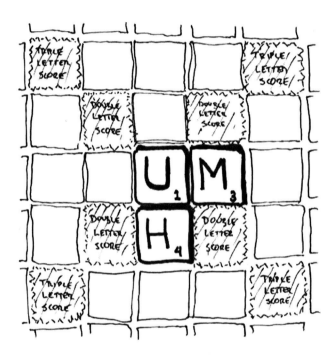

IDIOT SCRABBLE

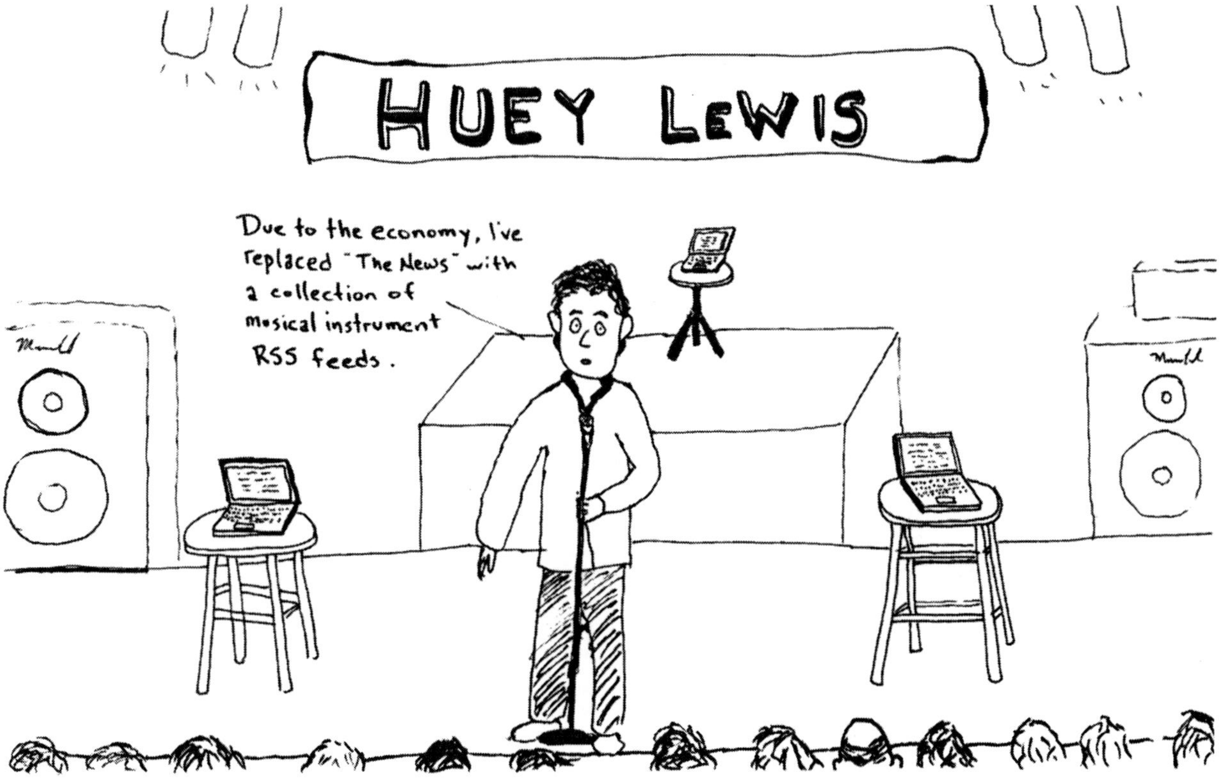
HUEY LEWIS
Due to the economy, I've replaced "The News" with a collection of musical instrument RSS feeds.

Bill The Belligerent Bunny Visits The Shady Pines Pre-School

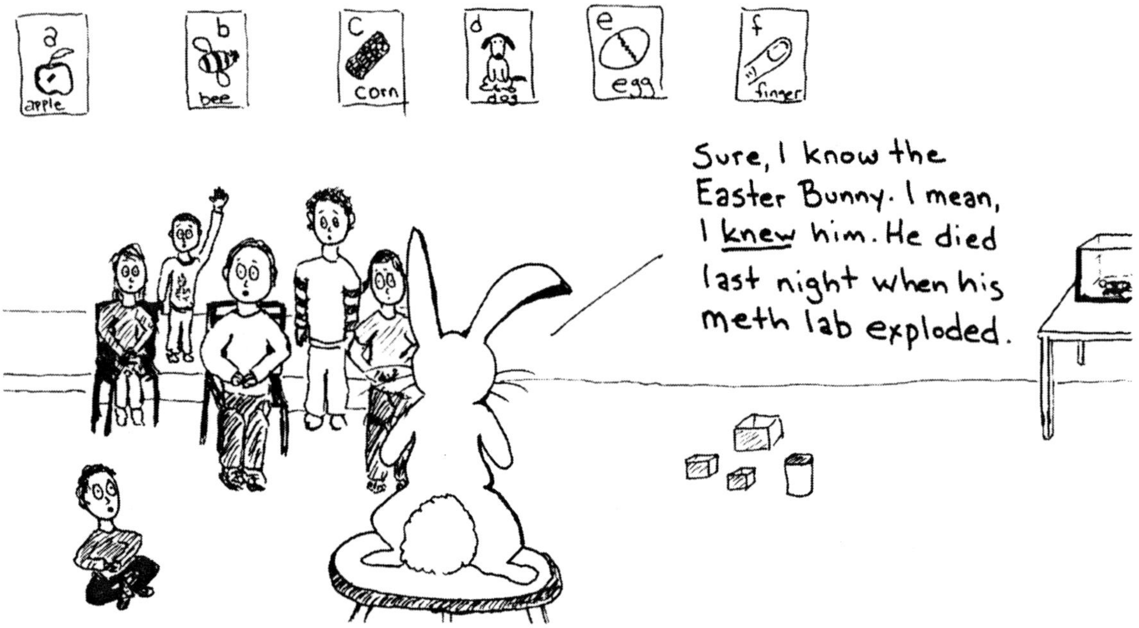
a
apple
b
bee
c
corn
d
dog
e
egg
f
finger
Sure, I know the Easter Bunny. I mean, I knew him. He died last night when his meth lab exploded.

He had every app
but the one
he wanted most.

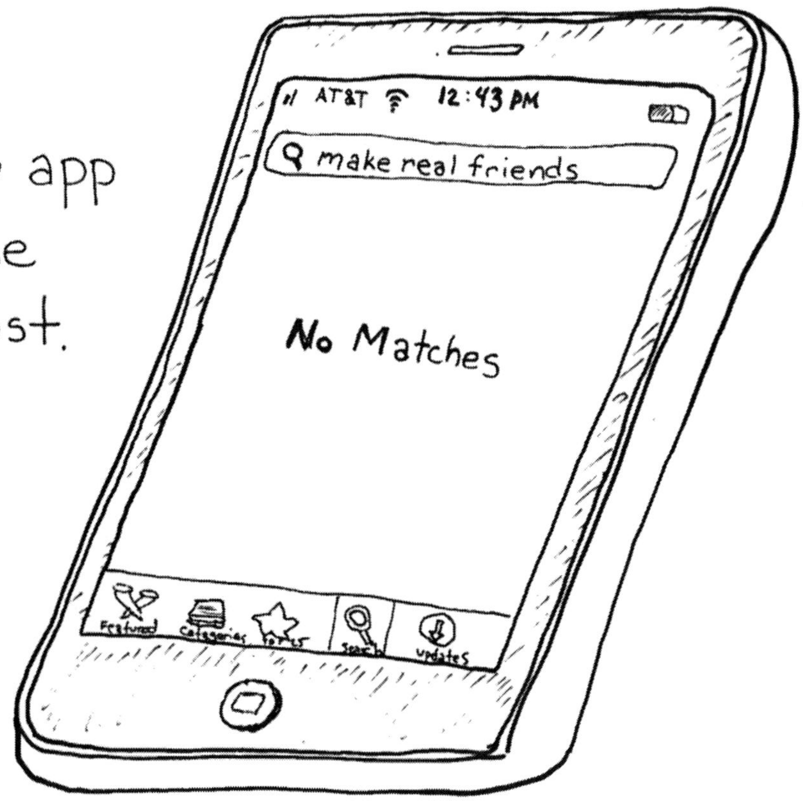
AT&T
12:43 PM
make real friends
No Matches
Featured
Categories
Top 25
Search
Updates

HELLO KITTY KNOCKOFFS
1930-1990

HEIL KITLER

1930s GERMANY

BONJOUR BAGUETTE

1960s FRANCE

YO, KAT!!!

1990s U.S.A.

When life gives you kale,
make kale and potato gratin.

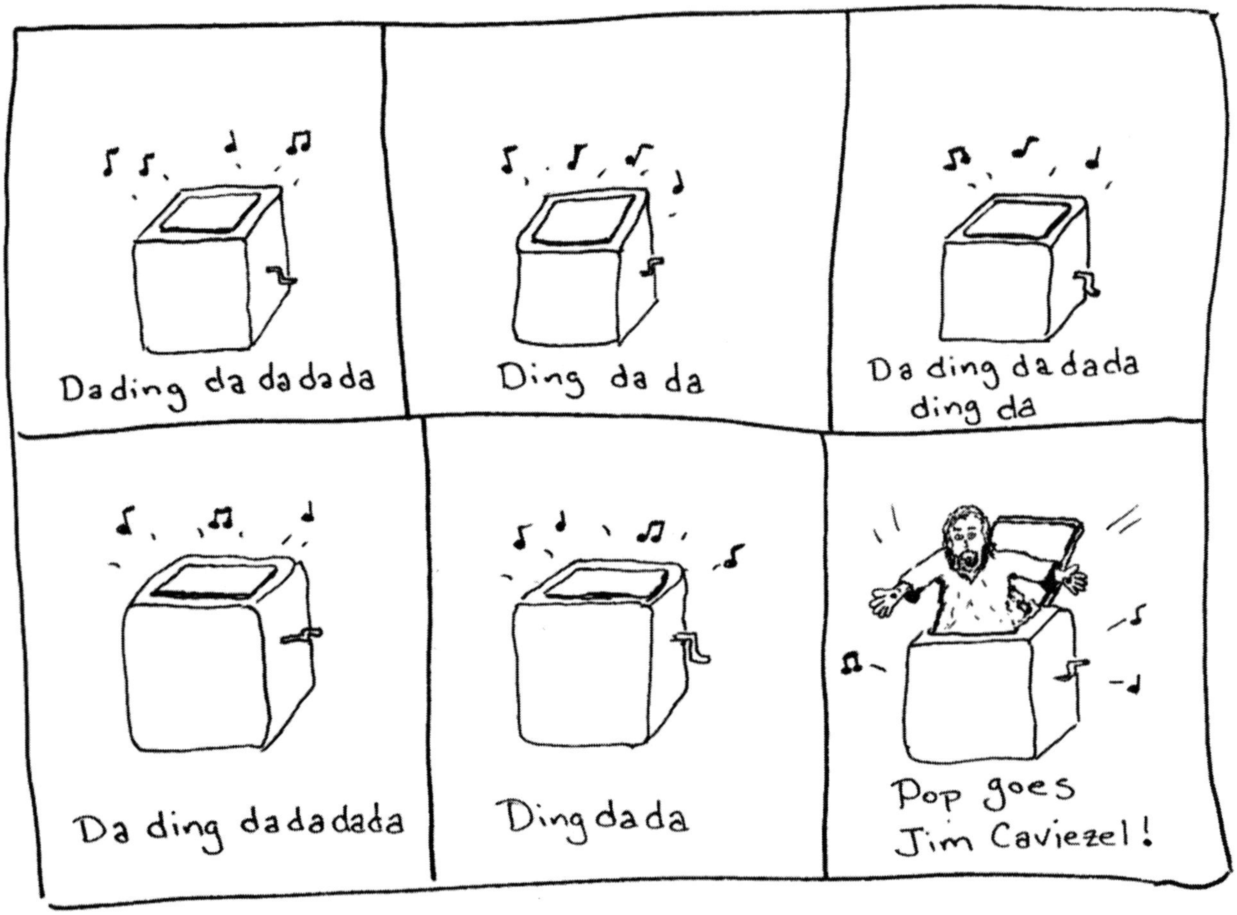
Da ding da dadada
Ding da da
Da ding dadada
ding da
Da ding dadadada
Ding dada
Pop goes
Jim Caviezel!

Sad Haiku: Cats

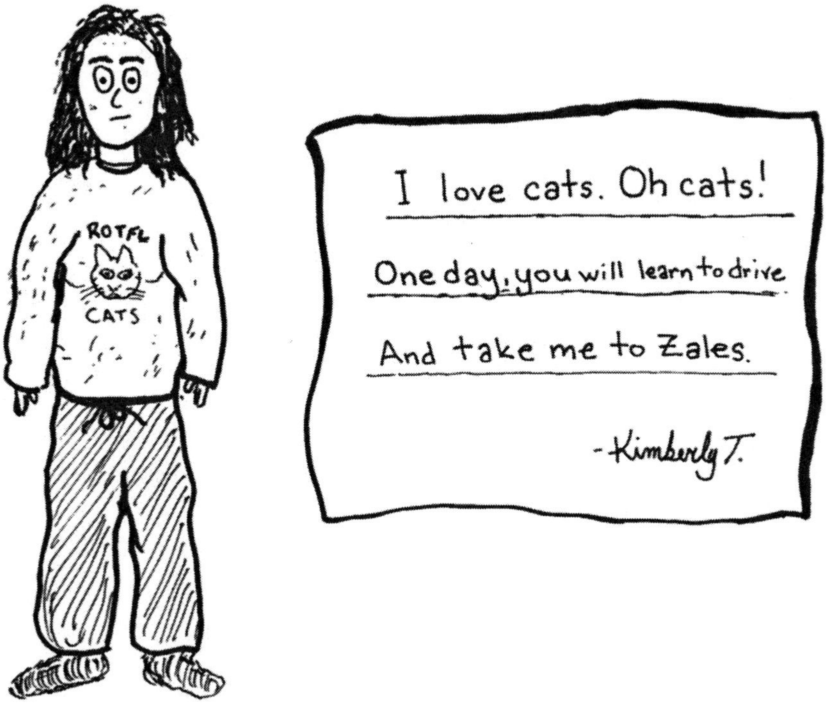
ROTFL
CATS
I love cats. Oh cats!
One day, you will learn to drive
And take me to Zales.
-Kimberly T.

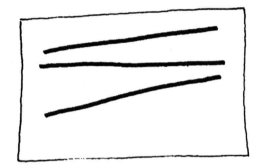

Potential uses:

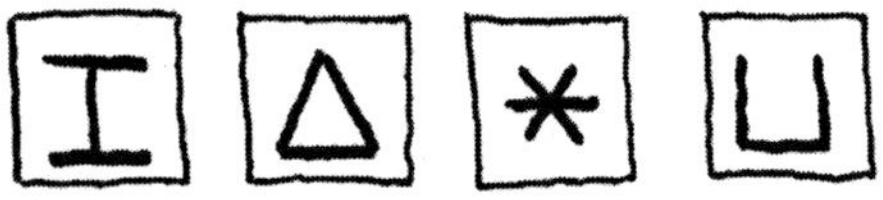

Lines (set of three)

$15.99

In stock

Classic, timeless, and incredibly versatile, lines are perfect for any age.

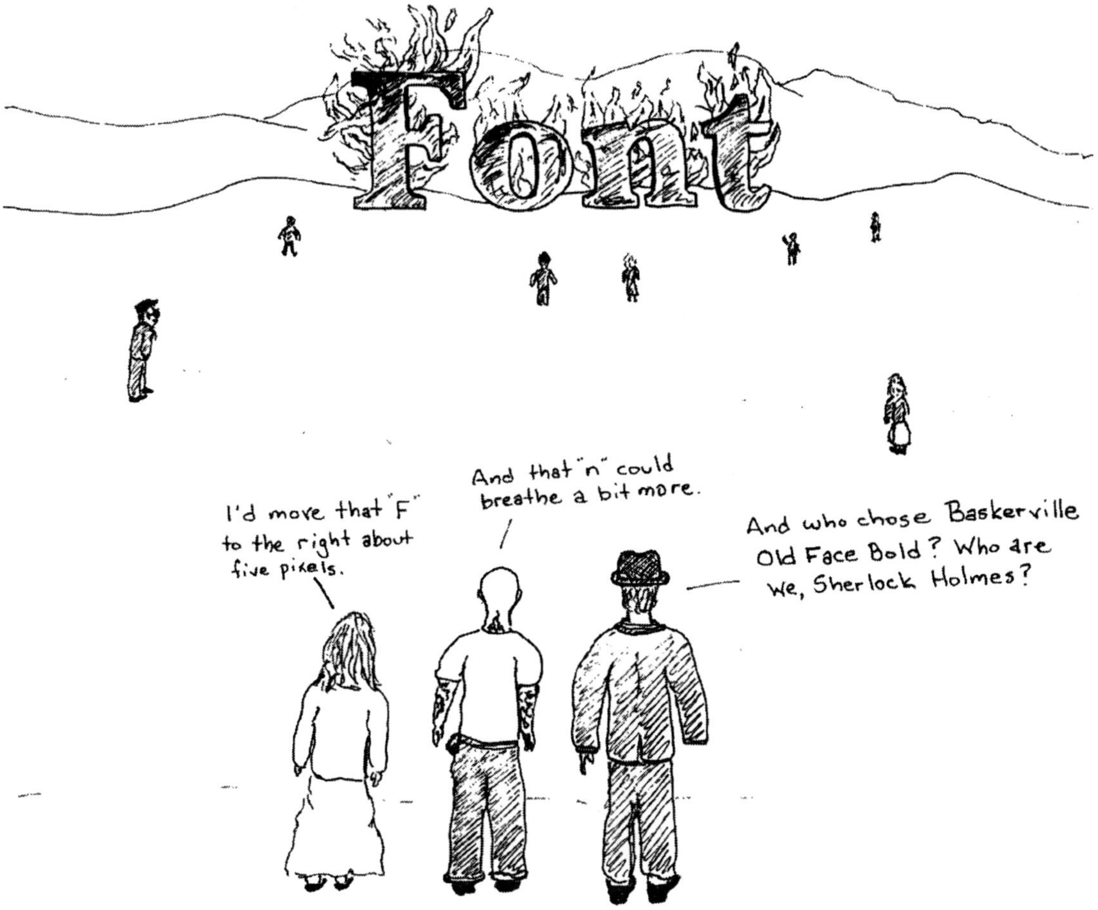
Font
I'd move that "F" to the right about five pixels.
And that "n" could breathe a bit more.
And who chose Baskerville Old Face Bold? Who are we, Sherlock Holmes?

Kerning Man

LOST

- My DIGNITY
- My PRIDE
- My LAST CONNECTION TO THE ANIMAL KINGDOM

If Found, Contact "Shia LaWoof" @ 555-1121

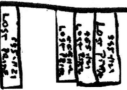

MICHAEL WASN'T LIKE THE OTHER KIDS.
HE WORE GLASSES.

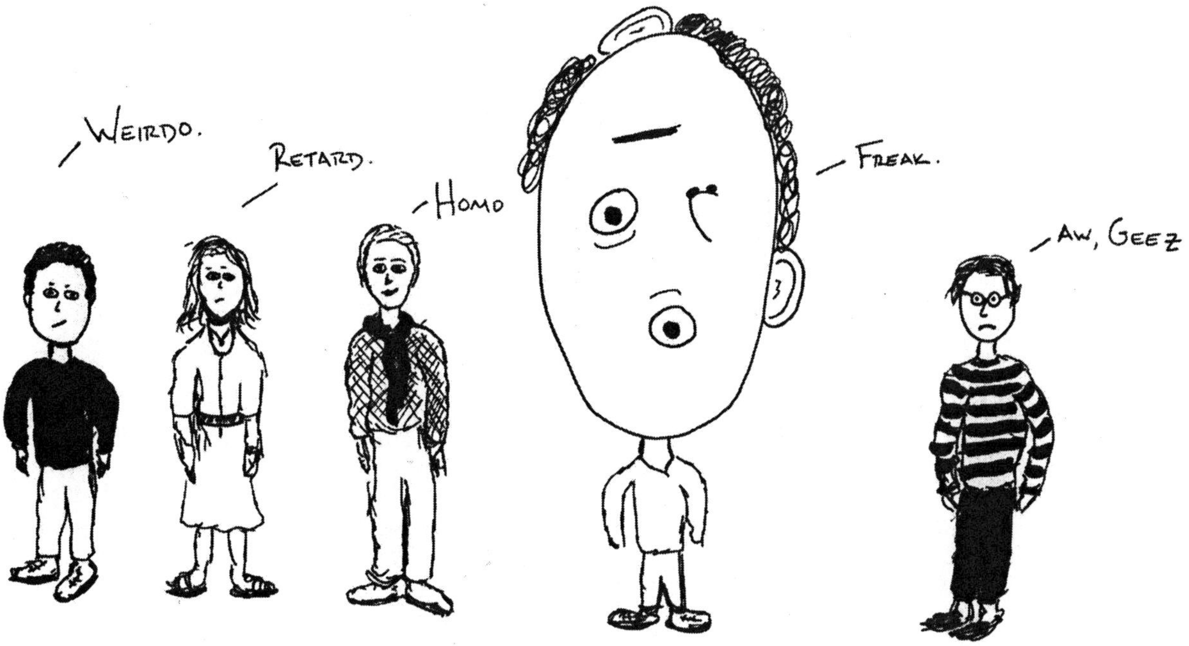
WEIRDO.
RETARD.
HOMO
FREAK.
AW, GEEZ

DURACELL

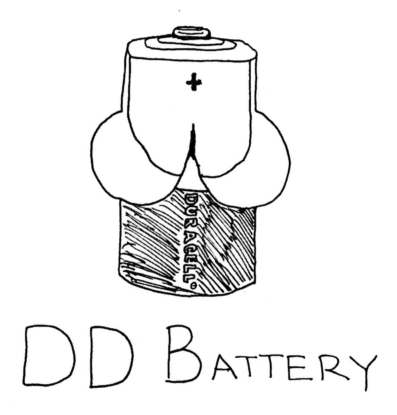

DD BATTERY

THINGS I WAS GOOD AT GROWING UP

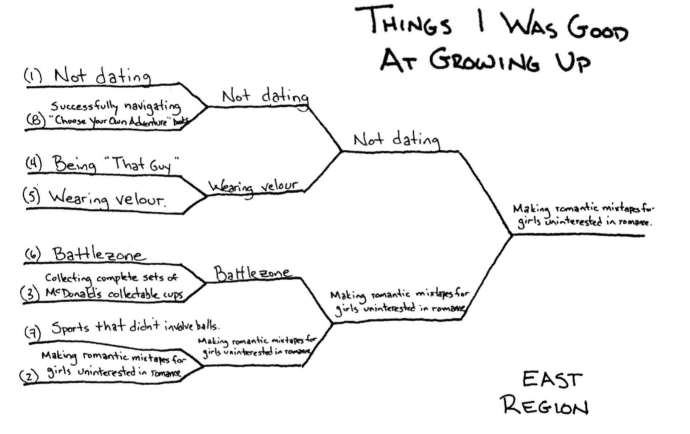

(1) Not dating

Not dating

(8) Successfully navigating "Choose Your Own Adventure" books

Not dating

(4) Being "That Guy"

(5) Wearing velour.

Wearing velour

Making romantic mixtapes for girls uninterested in romance.

(6) Battlezone

Battlezone

(3) Collecting complete sets of McDonald's collectable cups

Making romantic mixtapes for girls uninterested in romance

(7) Sports that didn't involve balls.

Making romantic mixtapes for girls uninterested in romance

(2) Making romantic mixtapes for girls uninterested in romance

EAST
REGION

THE MALL OF YOUR LIFE

1st Floor

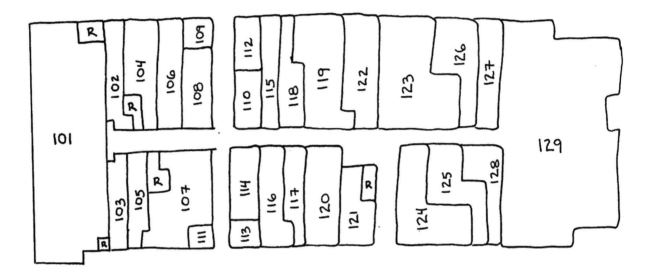

101	BABIES R' US	111	Sweet Things	121	Urban Outfitters
102	Baby Gap	112	Lids	122	Victoria's Secret
103	The Children's Place	113	Orange Julius	123	H & M
104	Gymboree	114	Johnny Rockets	124	PF Chang's
105	Janie and Jack	115	Spencer's Gifts	125	Tony Roma's
106	Build-a-Bear	116	Wet Seal	126	Zales
107	TOYS R' US	117	Forever 21	127	Men's Wearhouse
108	American Girl	118	Hot Topic	128	David's Bridal
109	Gamestop	119	ABERCROMBIE & FITCH	129	MACY'S
110	Claire's	120	American Apparel	R	Restrooms

THE MALL OF YOUR LIFE
2ND FLOOR

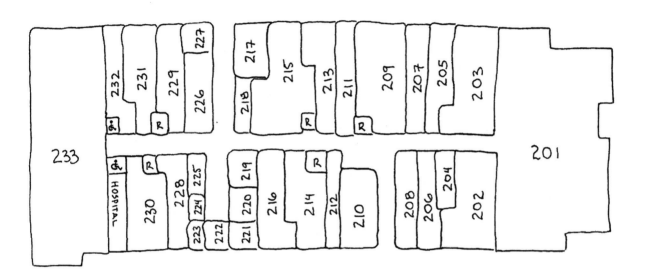

201 MACY's	211 Crew Cuts by J. Crew	221 Starbucks
202 J. Crew	212 Hanna Andersson	222 Teavana
203 Williams Sonoma	213 Gap Kids	223 Starbucks
204 Starbucks	214 Lenscrafters	224 Godiva
205 Banana Republic	215 KB Toys	225 Starbucks
206 Ann Taylor Loft	216 Tommy Bahama	226 Rockport
207 Starbucks	217 Harley Davidson	227 Talbots
208 Starbucks	218 The Ferrari Store	228 Lane Bryant
209 The Apple Store	219 Starbucks	229 Chico's
210 A Pea in the Pod	220 Aunt Annies	230 Harry and David
		231 La Z Boy
		232 See's candies

233 Walgreens

NOT SO EAGER BEAVER

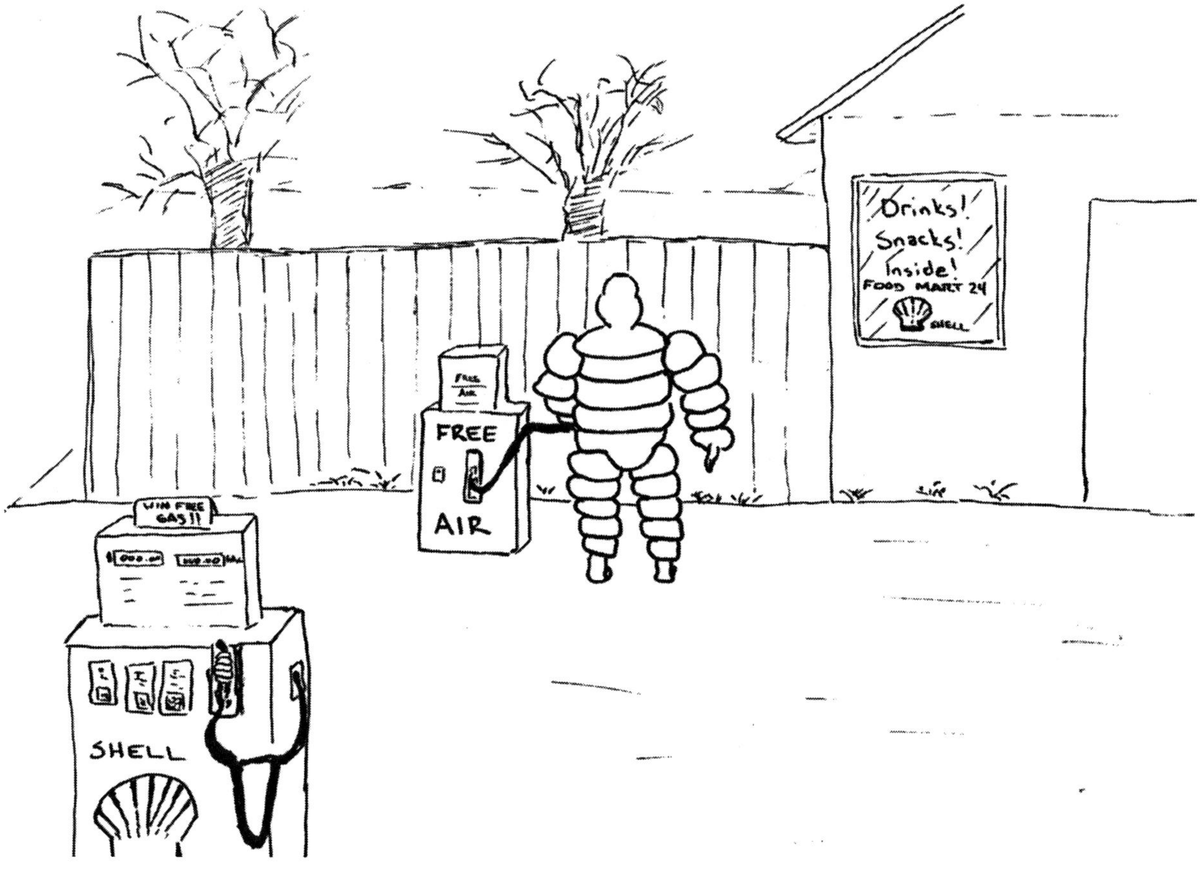
Drinks!
Snacks!
Inside!
FOOD MART 24
SHELL
FREE AIR
FREE
AIR
WIN FREE GAS!!
SHELL

Erectile Dysfunction Michelin Man

SAD HAIKU: BARNEY

Single, fifty, I'm
An Understudy for the
Barney on Ice tour.

- Mike

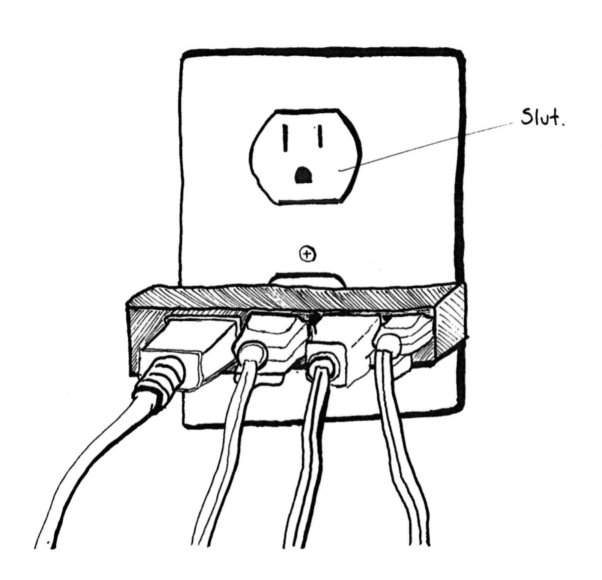

Slut.

WITHOUT HIS SIGNATURE MONOCLE AND KAZOO,
RAY WAS JUST ANOTHER PLAIN OLD MANATEE.

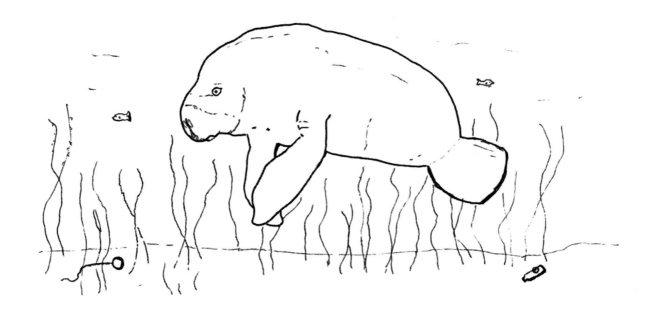

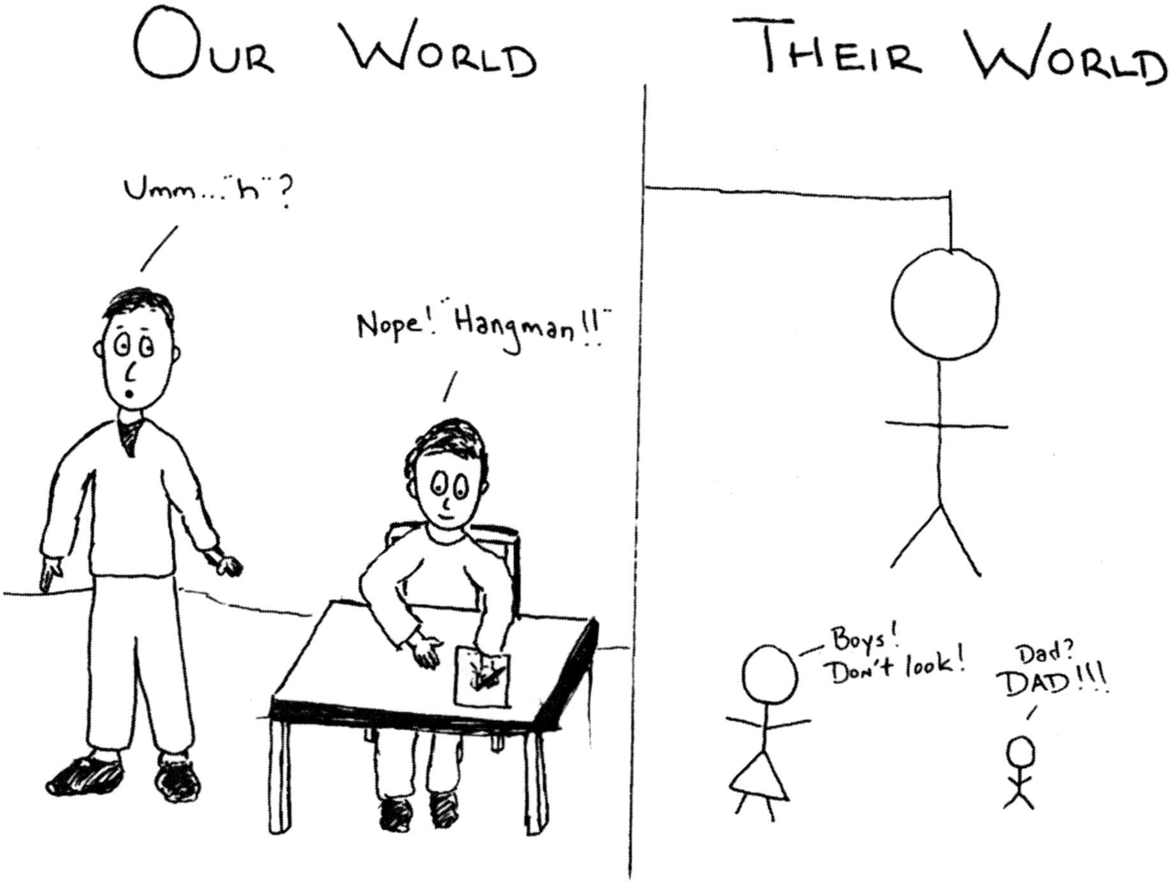

OUR WORLD
THEIR WORLD
Umm..."h"?
Nope! "Hangman!!"
Boys! Don't look!
Dad? DAD!!!
I'm gonna puke!

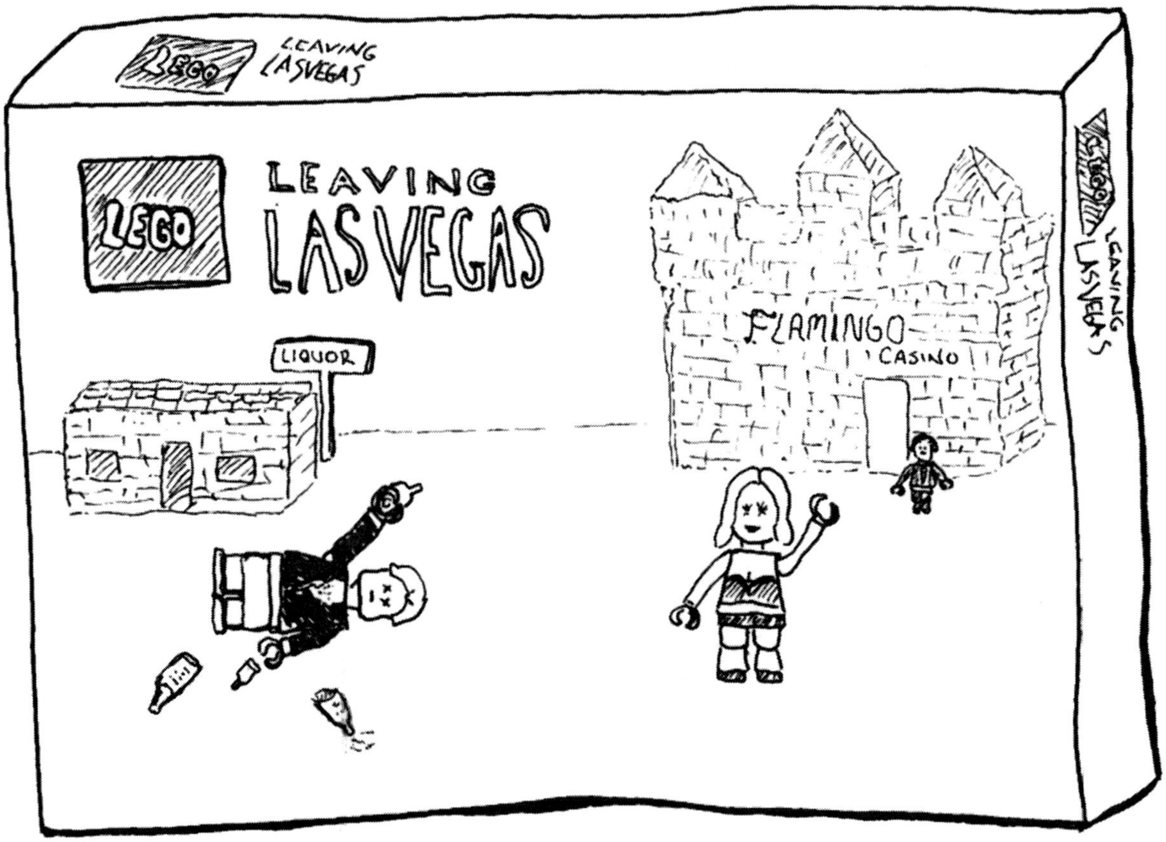
LEGO
LEAVING LAS VEGAS
LIQUOR
FLAMINGO
CASINO

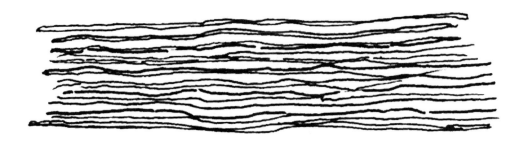

PAPER DOLL ORGY

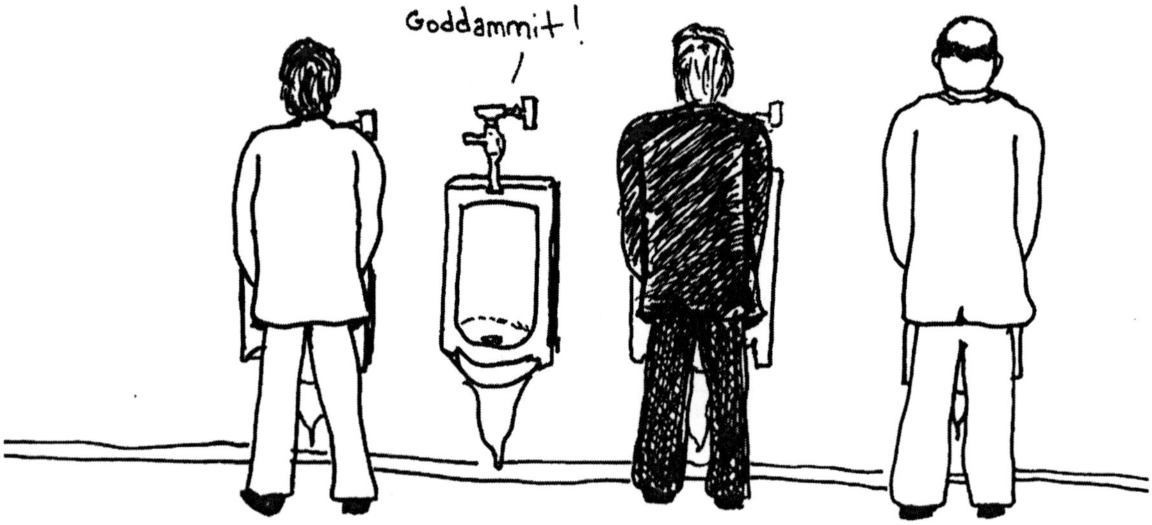
Goddammit!

WORST SHAPESHIFTER EVER

JOHN STRUGGLED WHEN IT CAME
TO SKETCHING "LADY PARTS."

ZONES

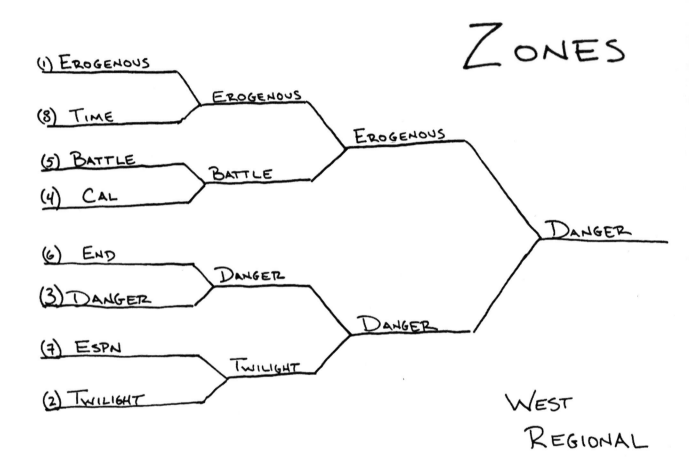

(1) EROGENOUS

(8) TIME

EROGENOUS

(5) BATTLE

(4) CAL

BATTLE

EROGENOUS

(6) END

(3) DANGER

DANGER

DANGER

(7) ESPN

(2) TWILIGHT

TWILIGHT

DANGER

DANGER

WEST
REGIONAL

pre-
natal
GAP

When in doubt,

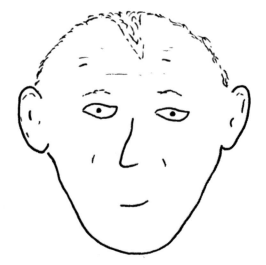

blame Phil Collins.

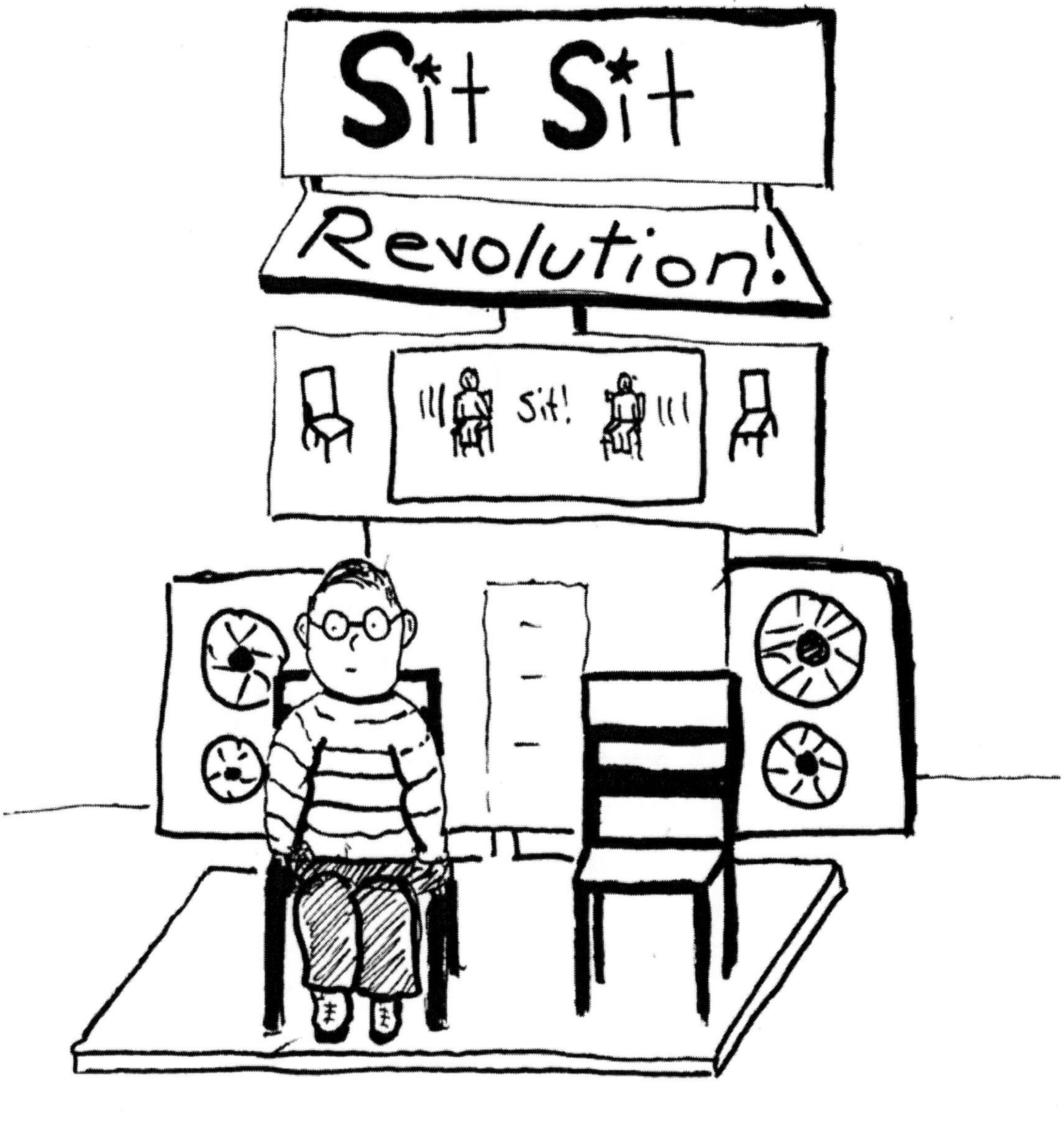
Sit Sit
Revolution!
Sit!

READ BETWEEN
hi!
THE LINES

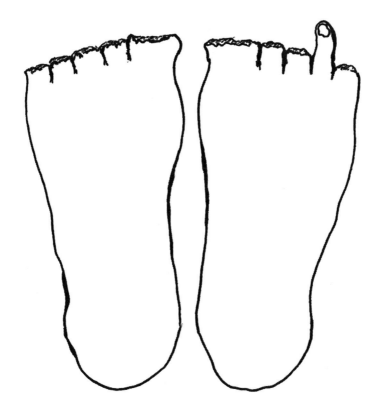

THIS LITTLE PIGGY WENT TO PRISON FOR LIFE
ON NINE COUNTS OF AGGRAVATED MURDER.

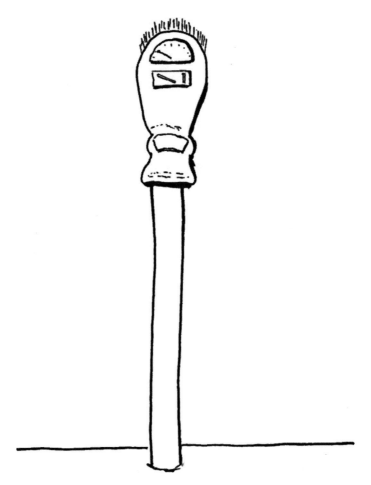

Brian Grazer
Parking Meter

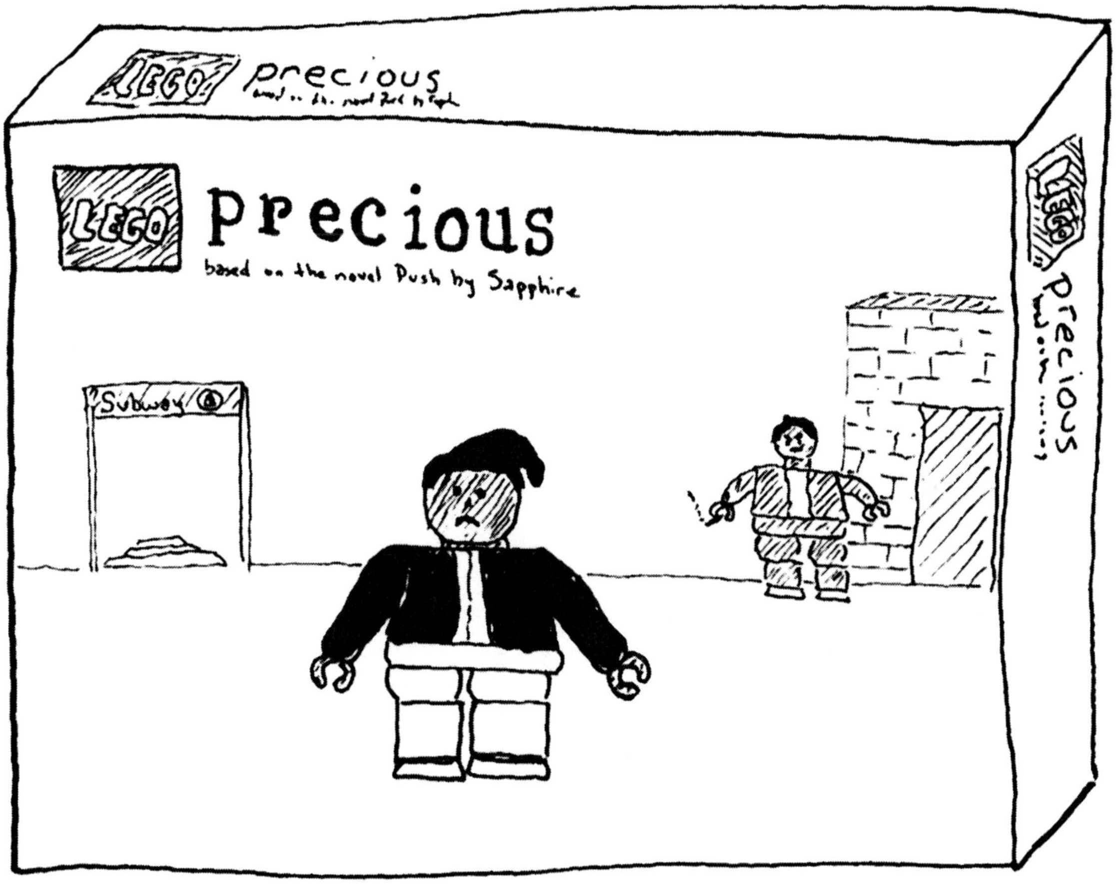
LEGO
precious
LEGO
precious
based on the novel Push by Sapphire
Subway
LEGO
precious

Things That Jimmy Cracked

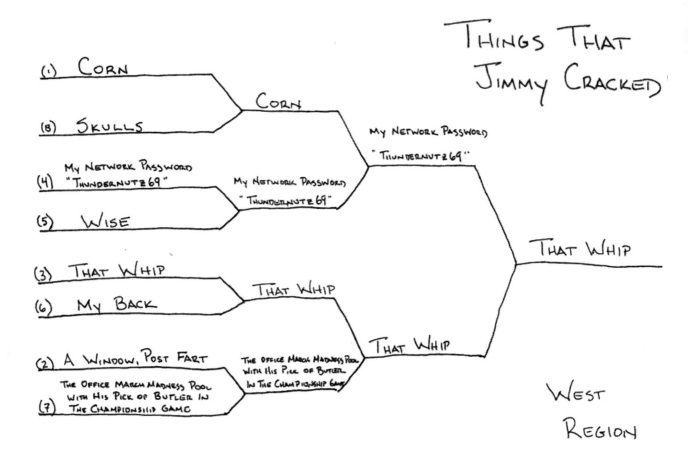

(1) CORN

(8) SKULLS

CORN

(4) My NETWORK PASSWORD "THUNDERNUTZ 69"

(5) WISE

MY NETWORK PASSWORD "THUNDERNUTZ 69"

MY NETWORK PASSWORD "THUNDERNUTZ 69"

(3) THAT WHIP

(6) MY BACK

THAT WHIP

THAT WHIP

(2) A WINDOW, POST FART

(7) THE OFFICE MARCH MADNESS POOL WITH HIS PICK OF BUTLER IN THE CHAMPIONSHIP GAME

THE OFFICE MARCH MADNESS POOL WITH HIS PICK OF BUTLER IN THE CHAMPIONSHIP GAME

THAT WHIP

THAT WHIP

WEST REGION

I WISH STATES WERE ROUNDER.

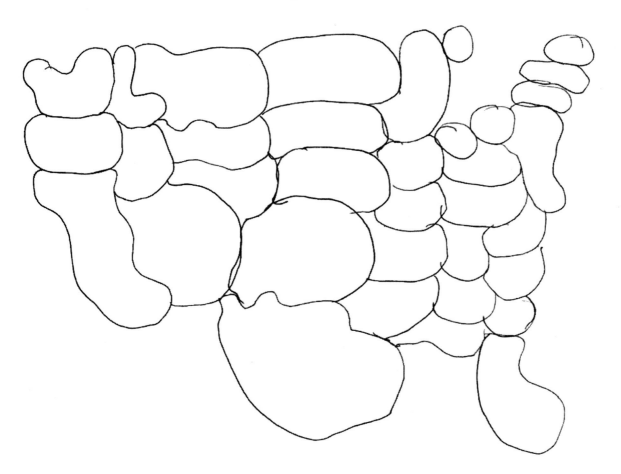

The fastest way from Point A to Point B?
Winged cheetah.

A   B

Rapunzel soon came to regret the new up-do

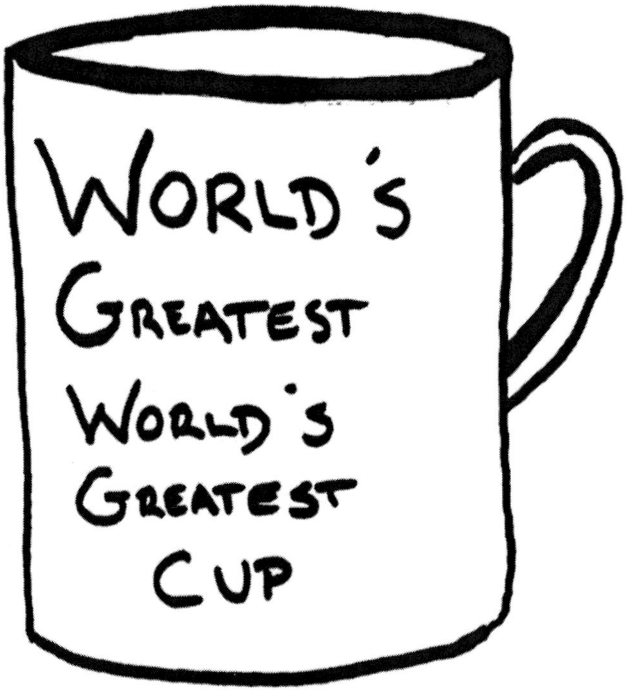
WORLD'S
GREATEST
WORLD'S
GREATEST
CUP

LABRADOUCHE

THE EVOLUTION OF TOOLS

SOPHIE'S CHOICE 2: SENIOR YEAR

FEAR NOT, SIR ROBERT, FOR TED CANNOT DRAW DRAGONS.

TIMMY FOSTER'S FIRST 100 DAYS

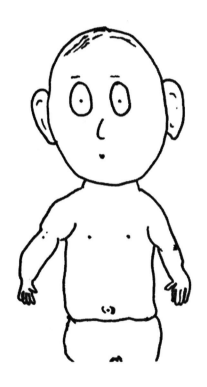

George F. Will: The economy is in ruins. We're stuck in two dead-end wars. And all the kid can do is play with his wiener. <u>C -</u>.

Peggy Noonan: 9 months of obsessive anticipation and what do we get? Poop and tears. <u>D</u>.

James Dobson: Worst. Baby. Ever. <u>F.</u>

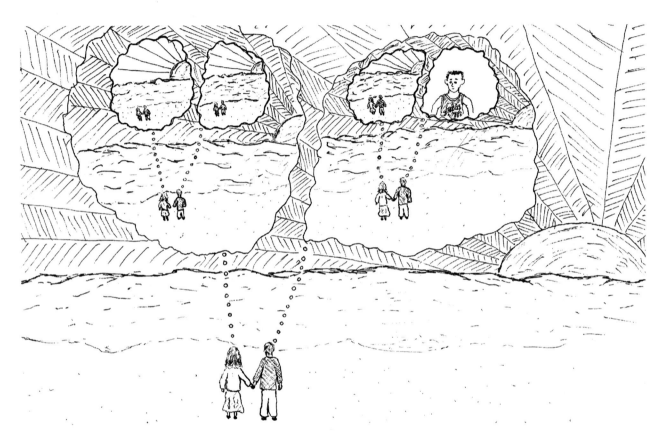

THINKING ABOUT THINKING ABOUT LOVE (AND DETLEF SCHREMPF)

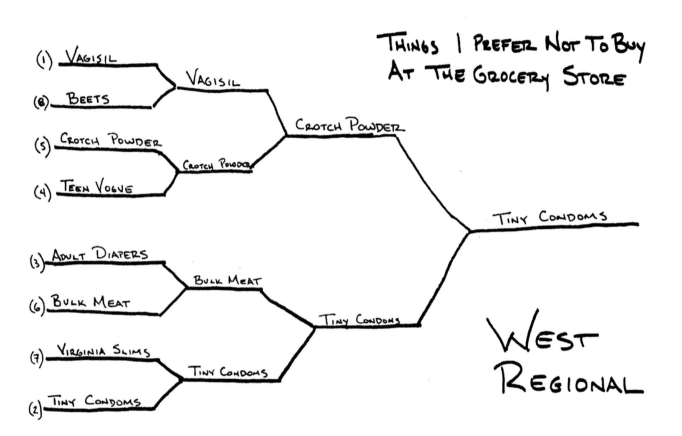

THINGS I PREFER NOT TO BUY
AT THE GROCERY STORE

(1) VAGISIL
(6) BEETS

VAGISIL

(5) CROTCH POWDER
(4) TEEN VOGUE

CROTCH POWDER

CROTCH POWDER

(3) ADULT DIAPERS
(6) BULK MEAT

BULK MEAT

TINY CONDOMS

(7) VIRGINIA SLIMS
(2) TINY CONDOMS

TINY CONDOMS

TINY CONDOMS

WEST
REGIONAL

She's Like The Wind

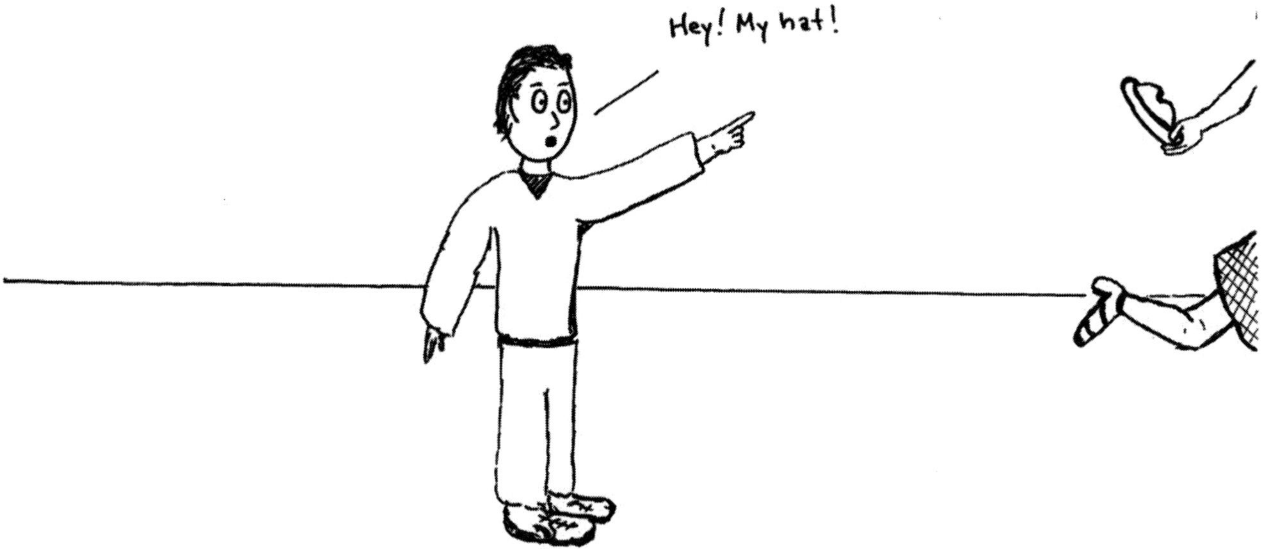
Hey! My hat!

Green Lake
Ballard
Laurelhurst
Queen Anne
Lake Union
Madison Park
Capitol Hill
Bellevue
Seattle Center
Lake Washington
Puget Sound
Downtown
Madrona
West Seattle
Mercer Island

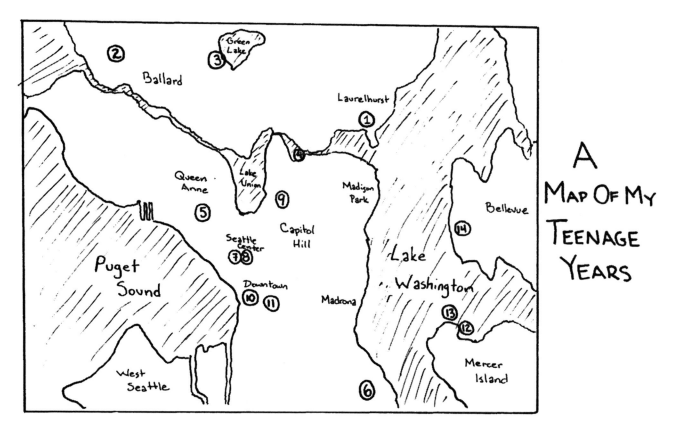

A Map Of My Teenage Years

1. First Kiss
2. First Sober Kiss
3. First Realization I Did Not Carry My Family's Athletic Genes.
4. First Beer.
5. First Run-in With The Law
6. First Bout With Self-Involved Teen Angst.
7. First Feeling of True Love.
8. First Feeling of Heartbreak.
9. First Unsuccessful Romantic Mix Tape given Away.
10. First Fake I.D. Purchased
11. First Time Vomiting Into A Hotel Planter
12. First Launching of Homemade Vessel.
13. First Sinking of Homemade Vessel.
14. First Prom Date Lost To Another Classmate.

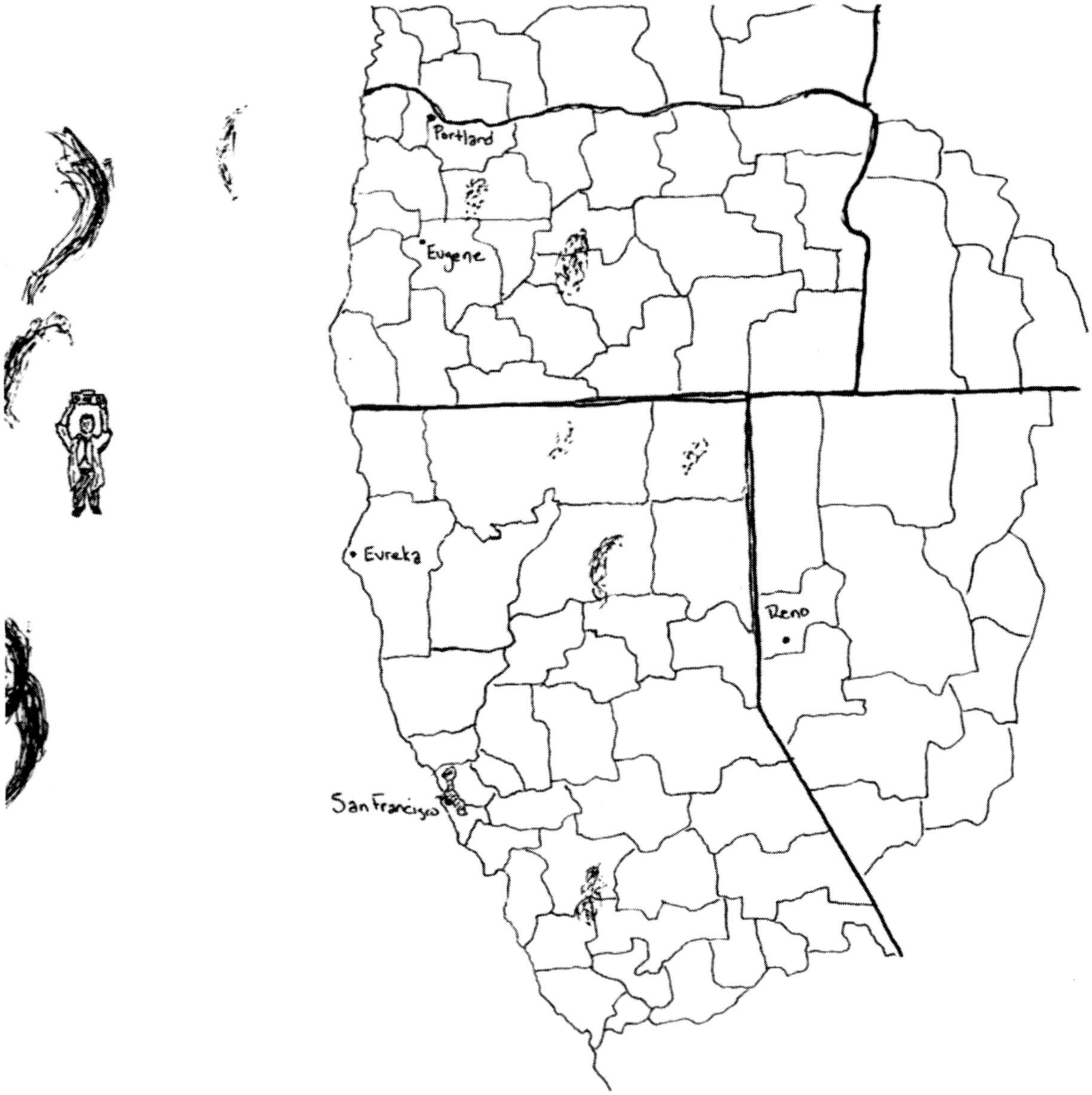
Portland
Eugene
Eureka
Reno
San Francisco

DOBLER RADAR

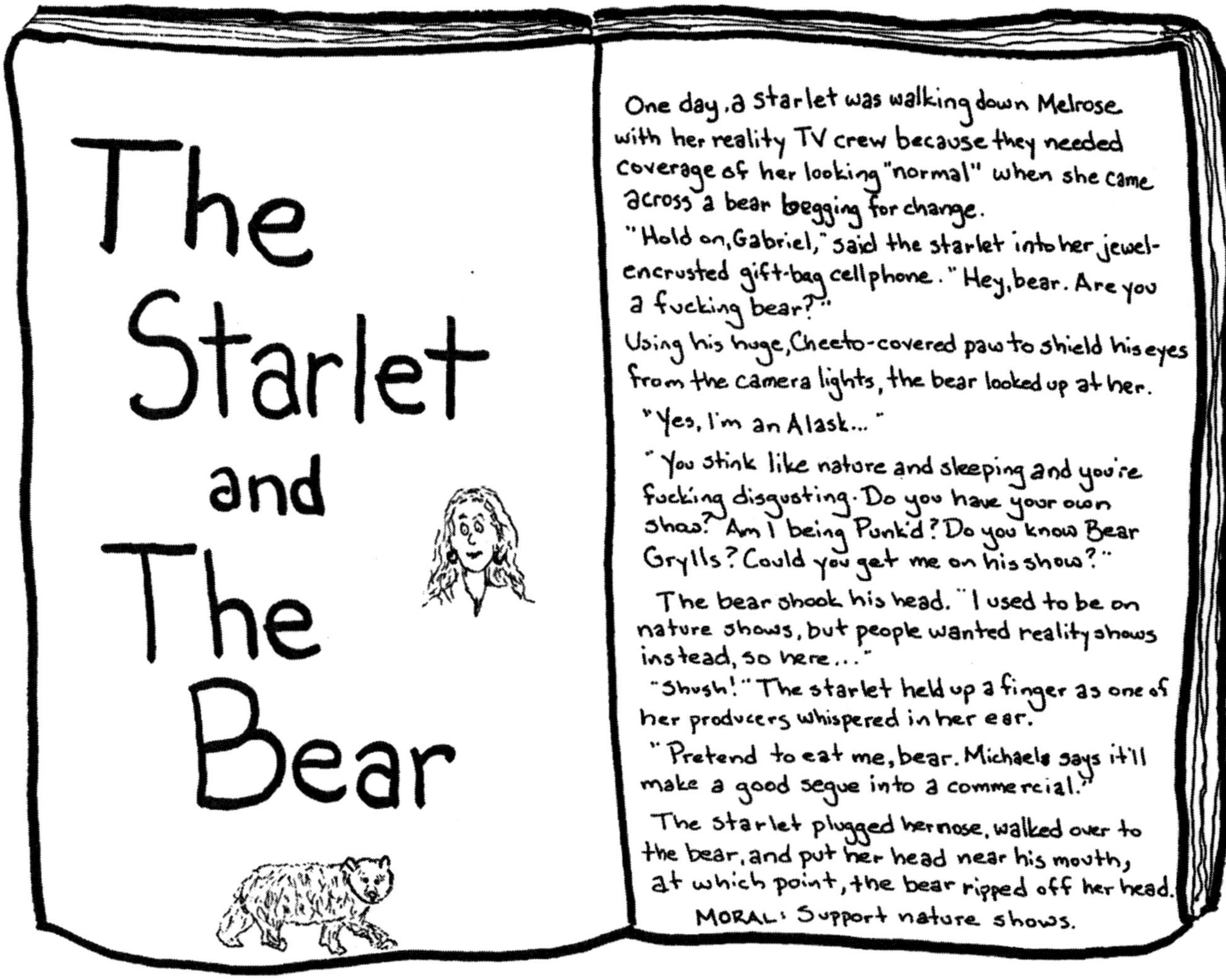
The Starlet and The Bear
One day, a starlet was walking down Melrose with her reality TV crew because they needed coverage of her looking "normal" when she came across a bear begging for change.
"Hold on, Gabriel," said the starlet into her jewel-encrusted gift-bag cellphone. "Hey, bear. Are you a fucking bear?"
Using his huge, Cheeto-covered paw to shield his eyes from the camera lights, the bear looked up at her.
"Yes, I'm an Alask..."
"You stink like nature and sleeping and you're fucking disgusting. Do you have your own show? Am I being Punk'd? Do you know Bear Grylls? Could you get me on his show?"
The bear shook his head. "I used to be on nature shows, but people wanted reality shows instead, so here..."
"Shush!" The starlet held up a finger as one of her producers whispered in her ear.
"Pretend to eat me, bear. Michaels says it'll make a good segue into a commercial."
The starlet plugged her nose, walked over to the bear, and put her head near his mouth, at which point, the bear ripped off her head.
MORAL: Support nature shows.

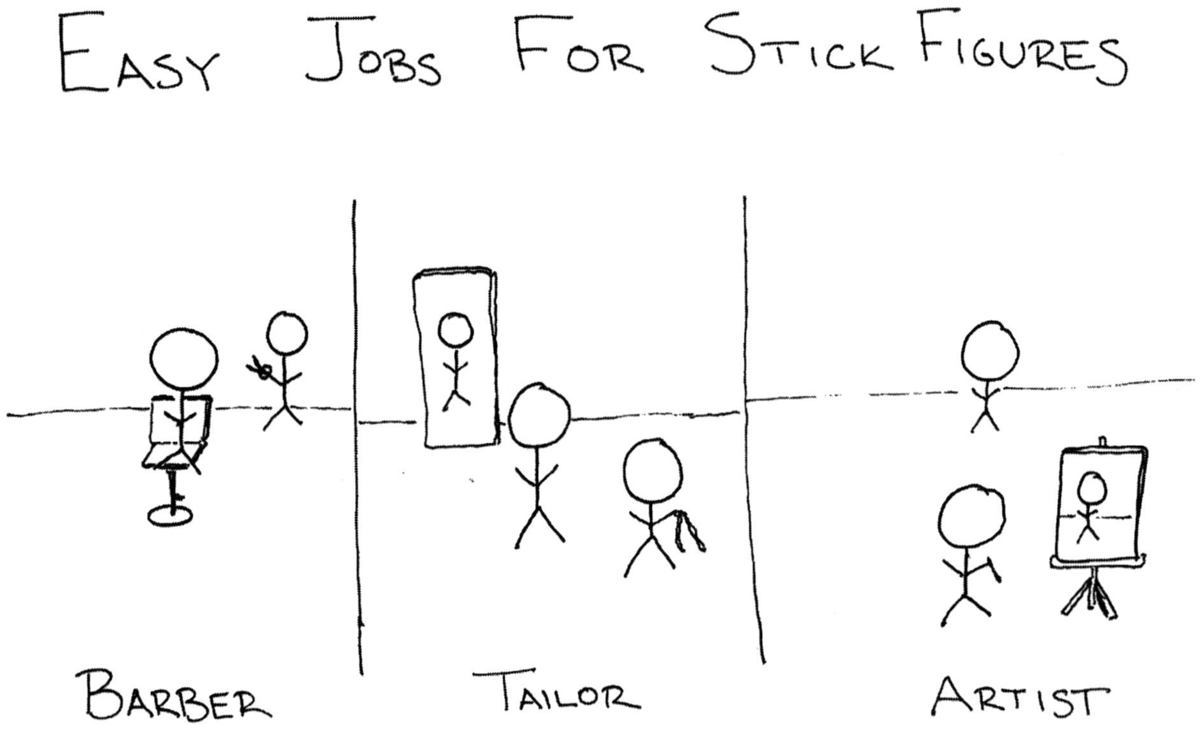
EASY JOBS FOR STICK FIGURES
BARBER
TAILOR
ARTIST

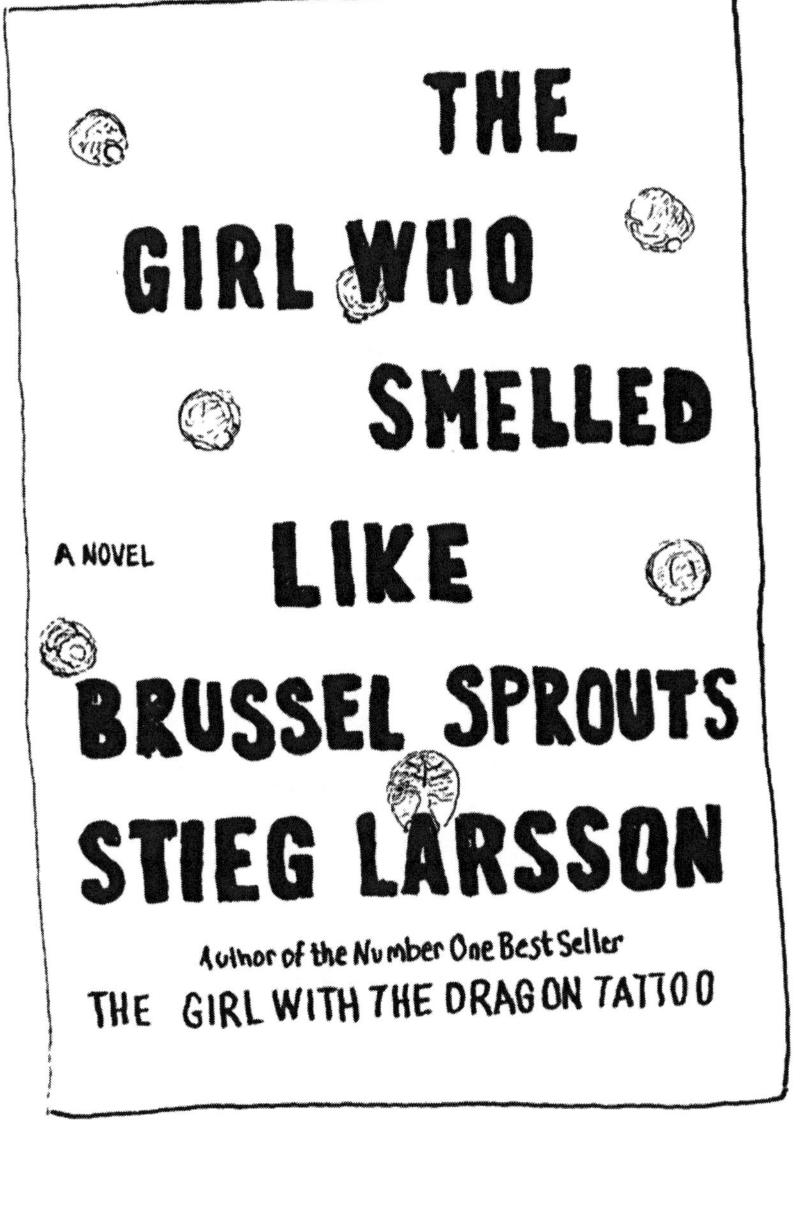
THE
GIRL WHO
SMELLED
A NOVEL
LIKE
BRUSSEL SPROUTS
STIEG LARSSON
Author of the Number One Best Seller
THE GIRL WITH THE DRAGON TATTOO

Cat Terror Threat Level

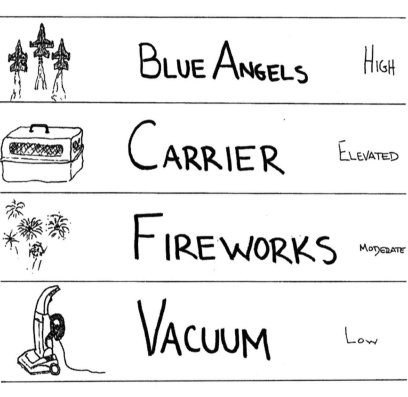

✈✈✈	Blue Angels	High
🧳	Carrier	Elevated
🎆	Fireworks	Moderate
	Vacuum	Low
	Costumes	Tolerable

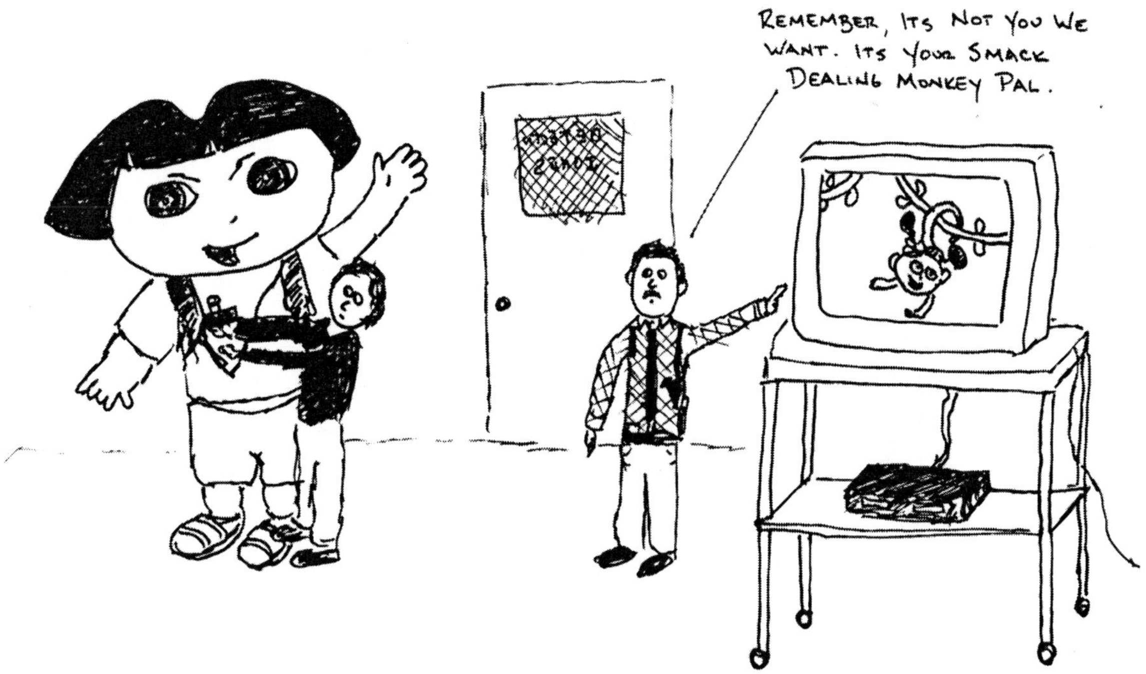
REMEMBER, ITS NOT YOU WE WANT. ITS YOUR SMACK DEALING MONKEY PAL.

DORA THE INFORMER

PLAY #57: THE GASSY QB

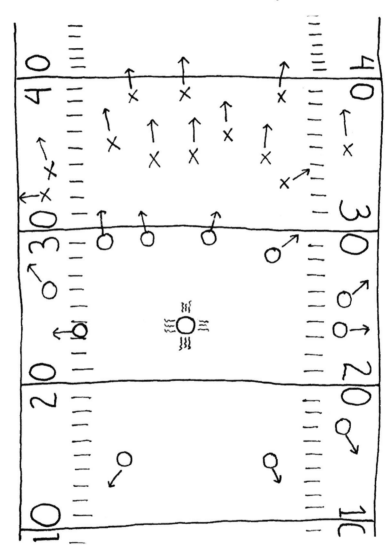

Nobody wins at Three Card Brontë

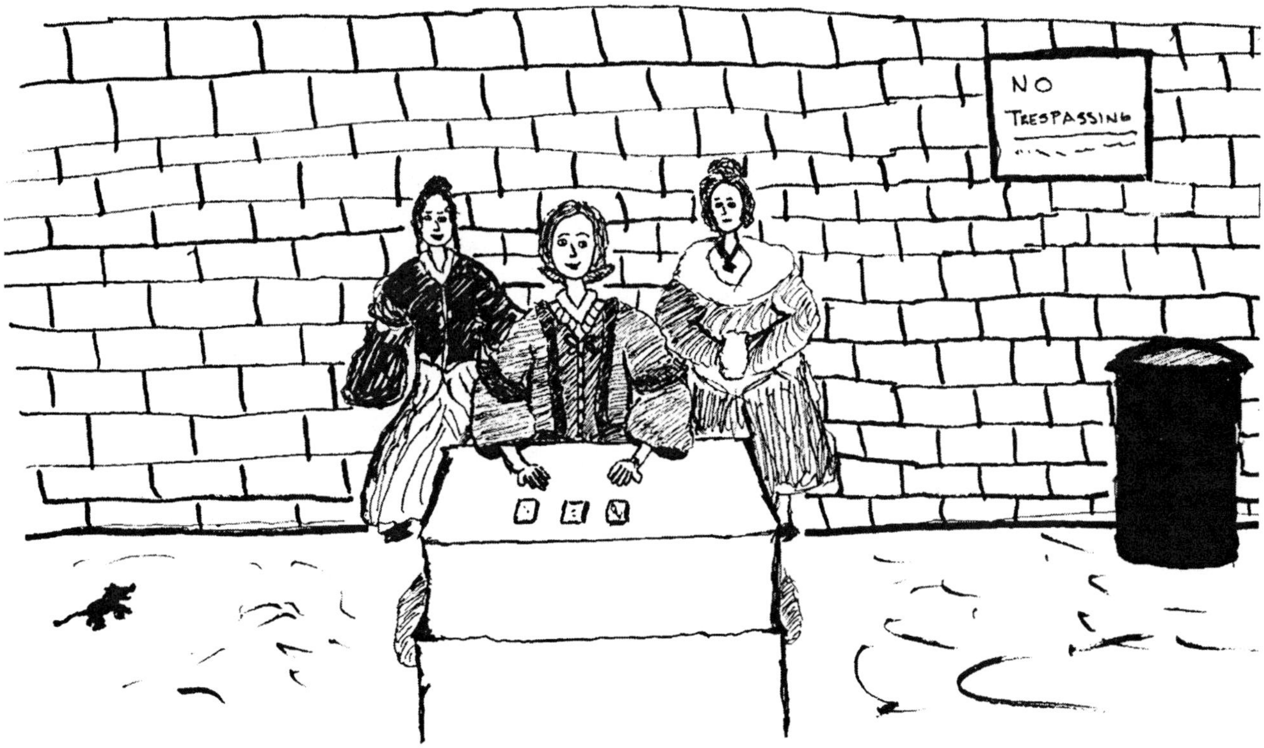
NO
TRESPASSING

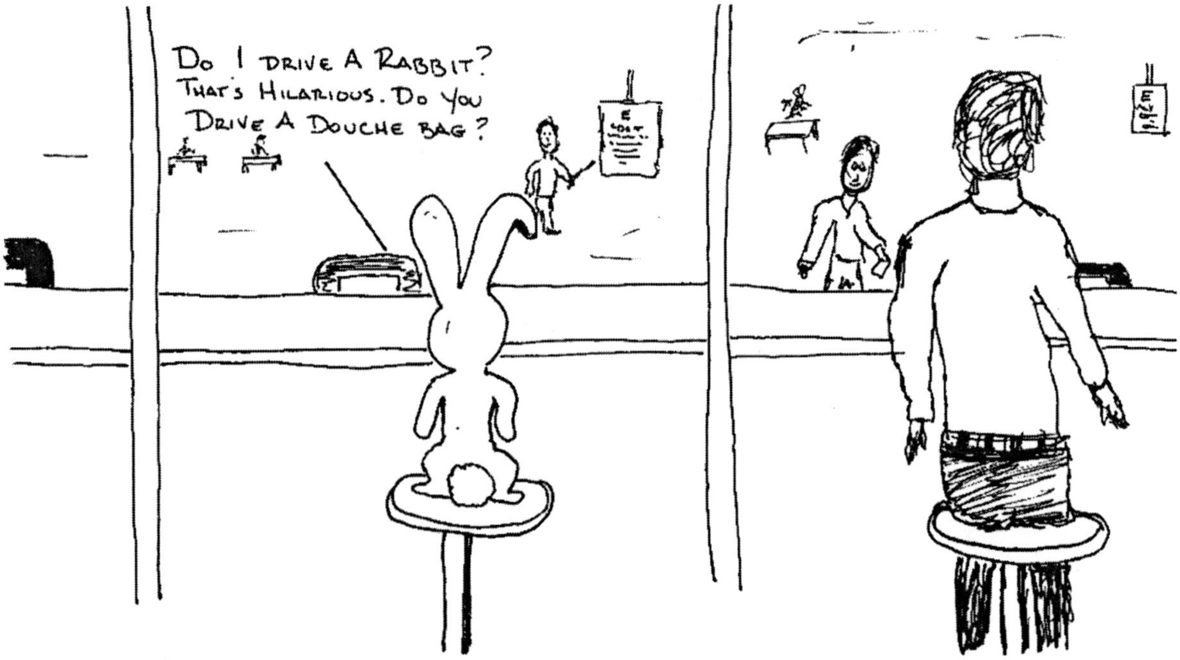
Do I drive a Rabbit?
That's Hilarious. Do You
Drive A Douche bag?

Bill The Belligerent Bunny
Visits The DMV

THE MOCK TURTLENECK

— Nice cardigan.

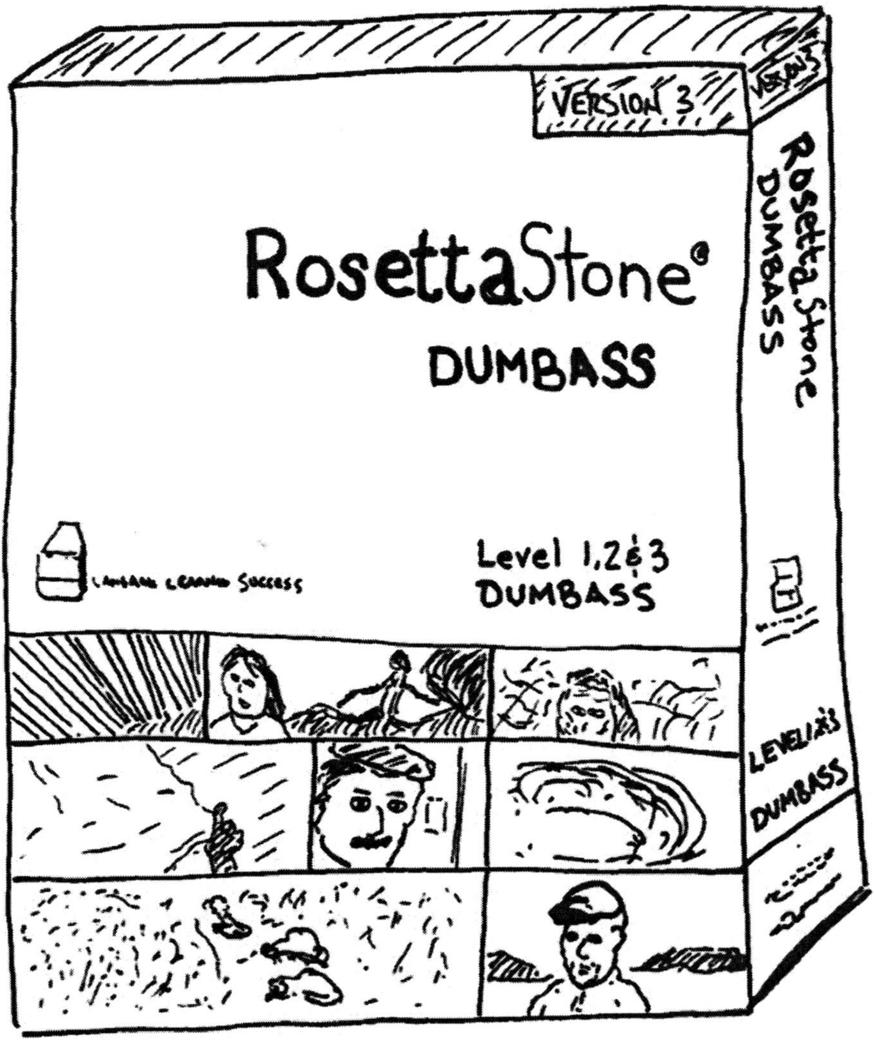
VERSION 3
RosettaStone®
DUMBASS
Level 1,2&3
DUMBASS
RosettaStone
DUMBASS
LEVEL1,2&3
DUMBASS

The amendment making it legal to eat other
committee members failed by a 4 to 1 margin.

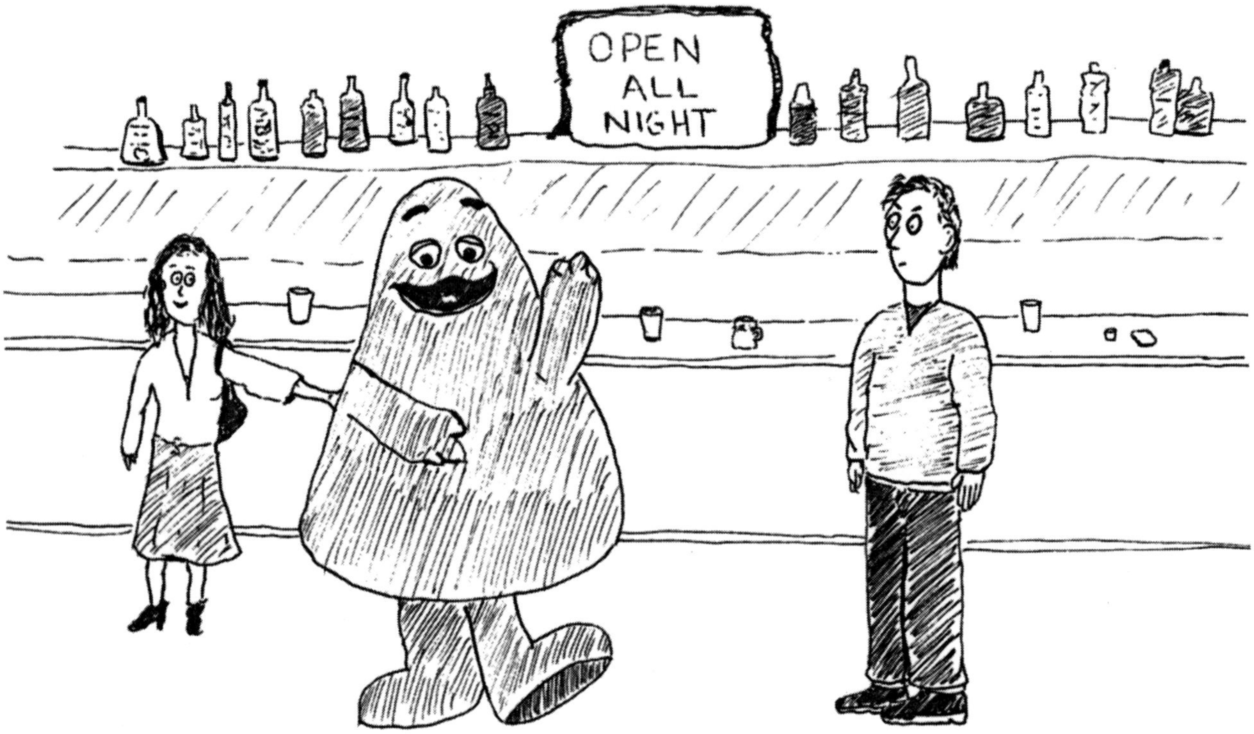
OPEN
ALL
NIGHT

Yet again, cockblocked by Grimace.

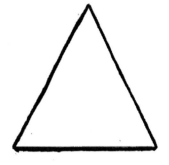

Dad, there's something I need to tell you. I'm scalene.

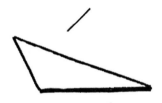

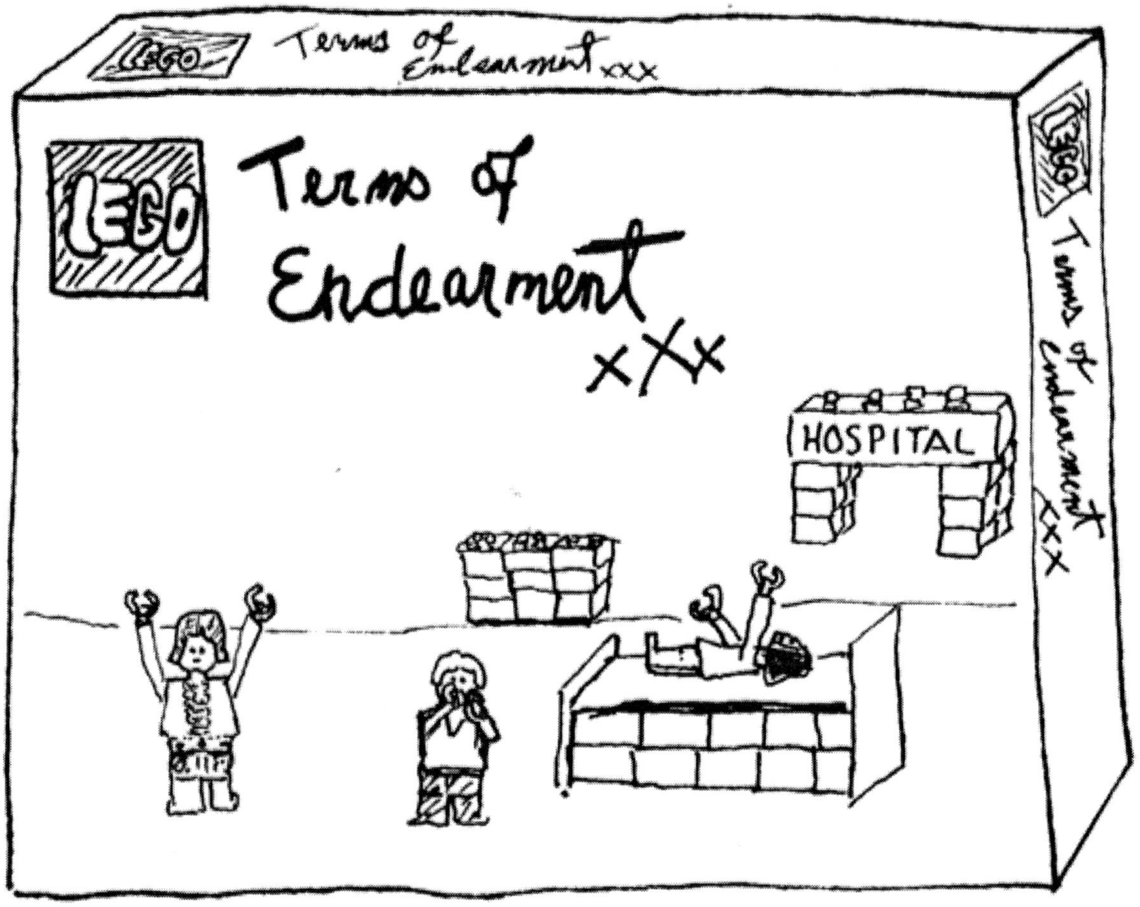
LEGO
Terms of Endearment xxx
LEGO
Terms of Endearment xxx
LEGO
Terms of Endearment xxx
HOSPITAL

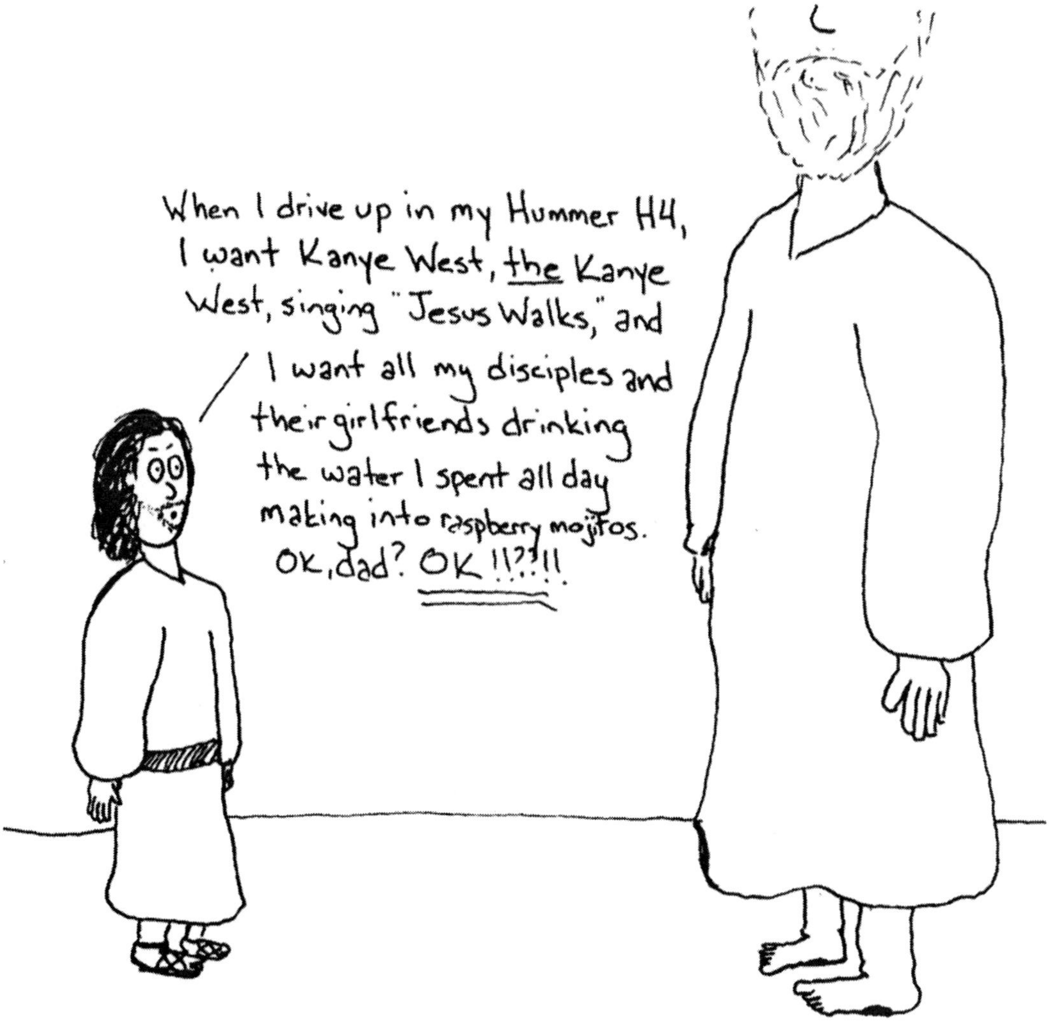
When I drive up in my Hummer H4, I want Kanye West, the Kanye West, singing "Jesus Walks," and I want all my disciples and their girlfriends drinking the water I spent all day making into raspberry mojitos. OK, dad? OK !!??!!

SUPER SWEET SIXTEEN

JESUS CHRIST

SAD HAIKU : MOVIE STAR

"You look like a star."
"Which?" I blushed. "That lady who
Played Gilbert Grape's mom."

— Erika

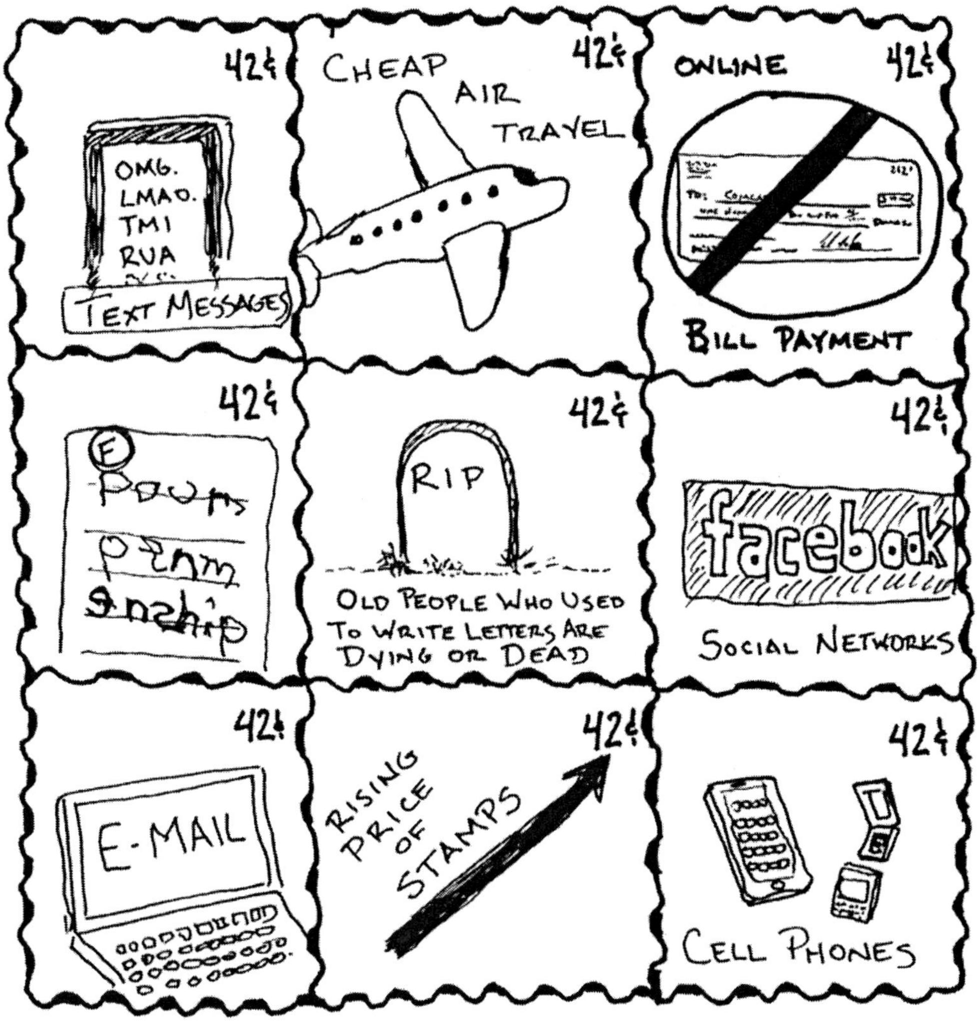
42¢
OMG.
LMAO.
TMI
RUA
Text Messages
42¢
Cheap Air Travel
42¢
Online Bill Payment
42¢
42¢
RIP
Old People Who Used To Write Letters Are Dying or Dead
42¢
facebook
Social Networks
42¢
E-MAIL
42¢
Rising Price of Stamps
42¢
Cell Phones

What Killed Postage Stamps Commemorative Postage Stamps

Mirror, mirror on the wall,
Where can I score some weed?

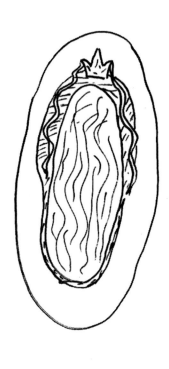

JUVIE SNOW WHITE

TOP CHEF : PRE-SCHOOL

I started with some freshly picked boogers, sautéed them with some stuff I found under a park bench, and seasoned it all with something from a region on my body my mommy calls "The Danger Zone."

Enjoy.

I GIVE TWO SHITS

There is a fine line
between irony and
total douchebaggery.

Act and dress with caution.

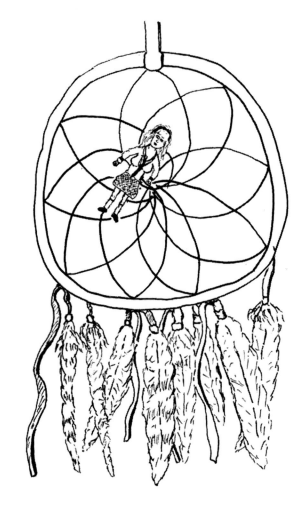

WET DREAM CATCHER

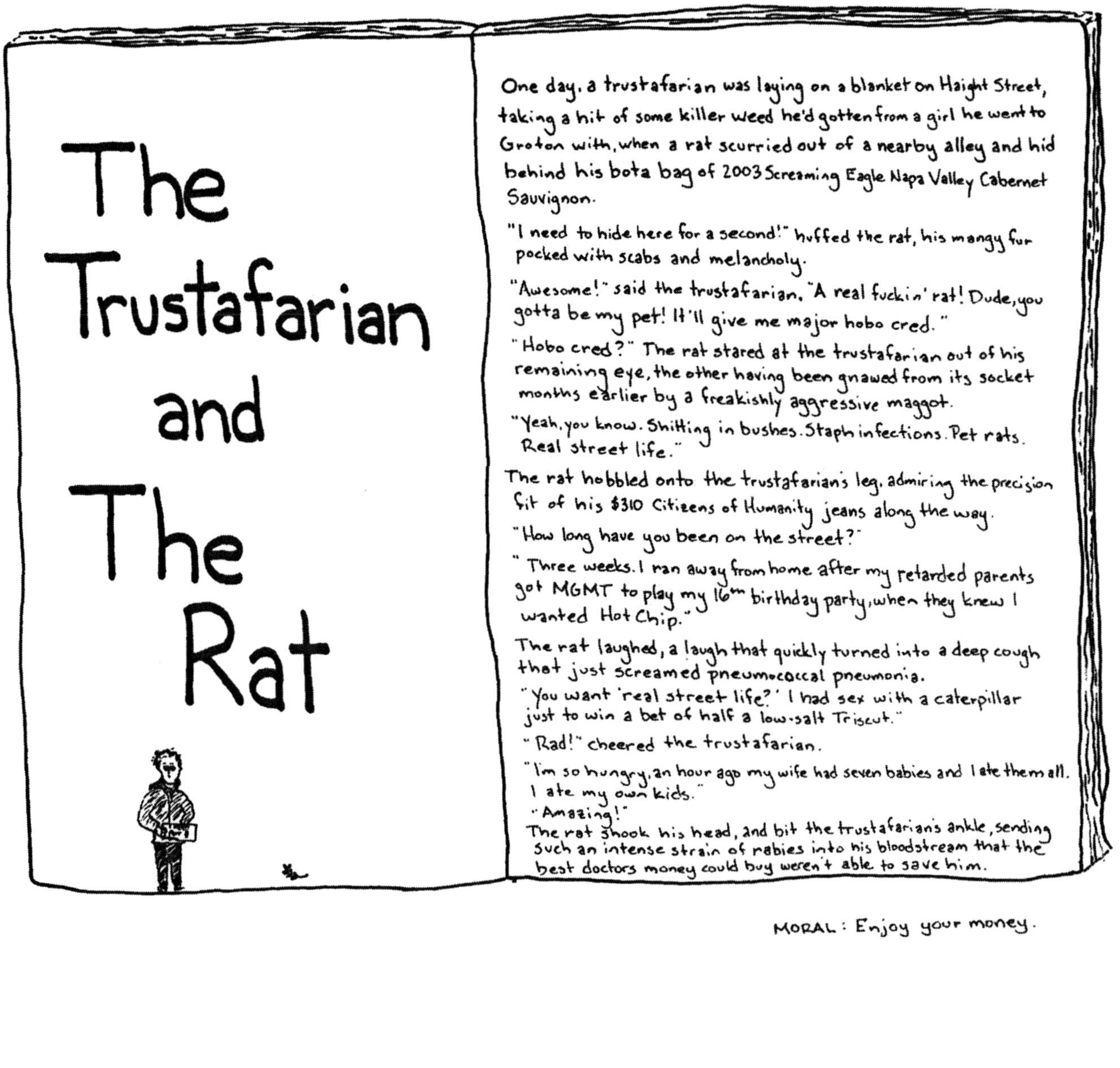

The Trustafarian and The Rat

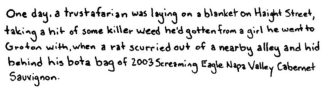

One day, a trustafarian was laying on a blanket on Haight Street, taking a hit of some killer weed he'd gotten from a girl he went to Groton with, when a rat scurried out of a nearby alley and hid behind his bota bag of 2003 Screaming Eagle Napa Valley Cabernet Sauvignon.

"I need to hide here for a second!" huffed the rat, his mangy fur pocked with scabs and melancholy.

"Awesome!" said the trustafarian. "A real fuckin' rat! Dude, you gotta be my pet! It'll give me major hobo cred."

"Hobo cred?" The rat stared at the trustafarian out of his remaining eye, the other having been gnawed from its socket months earlier by a freakishly aggressive maggot.

"Yeah, you know. Shitting in bushes. Staph infections. Pet rats. Real street life."

The rat hobbled onto the trustafarian's leg, admiring the precision fit of his $310 Citizens of Humanity jeans along the way.

"How long have you been on the street?"

"Three weeks. I ran away from home after my retarded parents got MGMT to play my 16th birthday party, when they knew I wanted Hot Chip."

The rat laughed, a laugh that quickly turned into a deep cough that just screamed pneumococcal pneumonia.

"You want 'real street life?' I had sex with a caterpillar just to win a bet of half a low-salt Triscuit."

"Rad!" cheered the trustafarian.

"I'm so hungry, an hour ago my wife had seven babies and I ate them all. I ate my own kids."

"Amazing!"

The rat shook his head, and bit the trustafarian's ankle, sending such an intense strain of rabies into his bloodstream that the best doctors money could buy weren't able to save him.

MORAL: Enjoy your money.

CORN DOG W/ DUNCE CAP

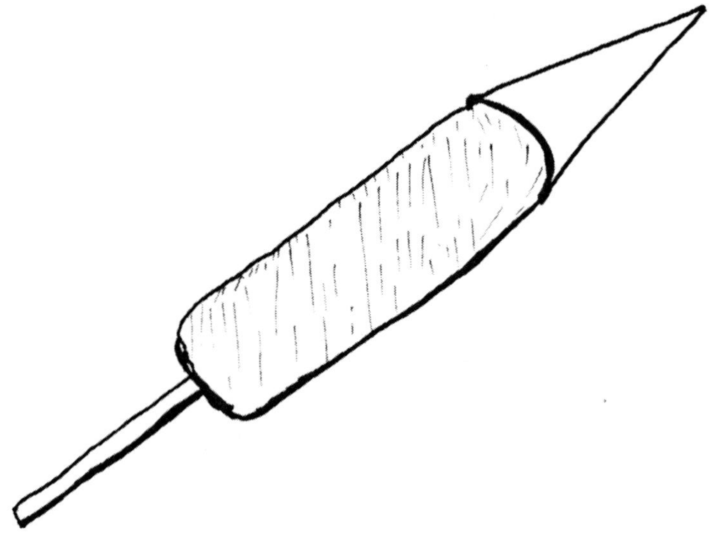

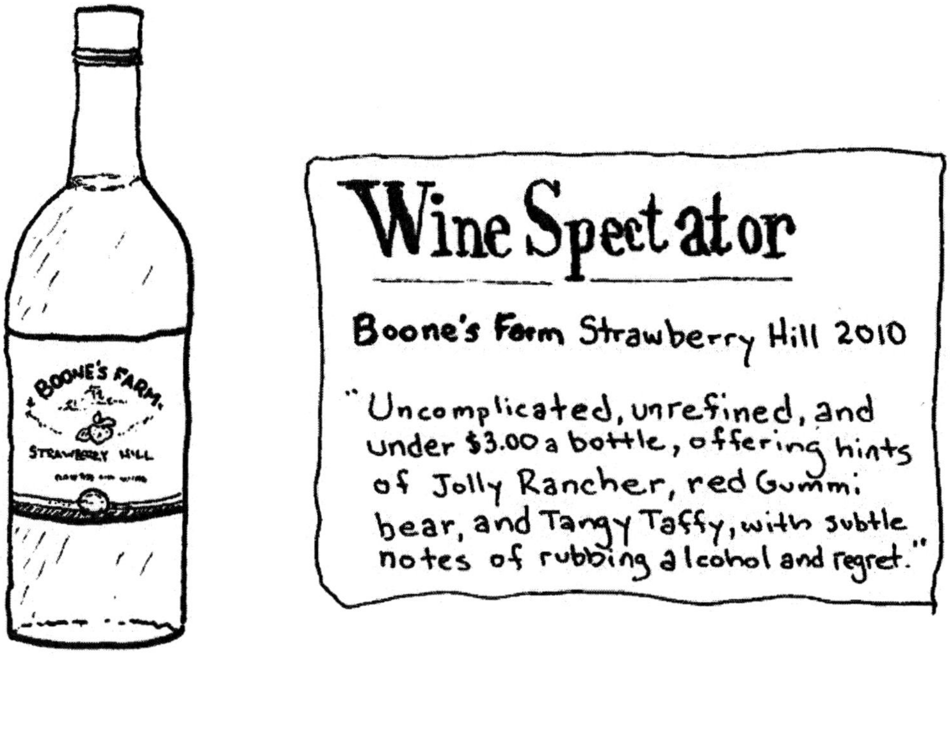
BOONE'S FARM
STRAWBERRY HILL
Wine Spectator
Boone's Farm Strawberry Hill 2010
"Uncomplicated, unrefined, and under $3.00 a bottle, offering hints of Jolly Rancher, red Gummi bear, and Tangy Taffy, with subtle notes of rubbing alcohol and regret."

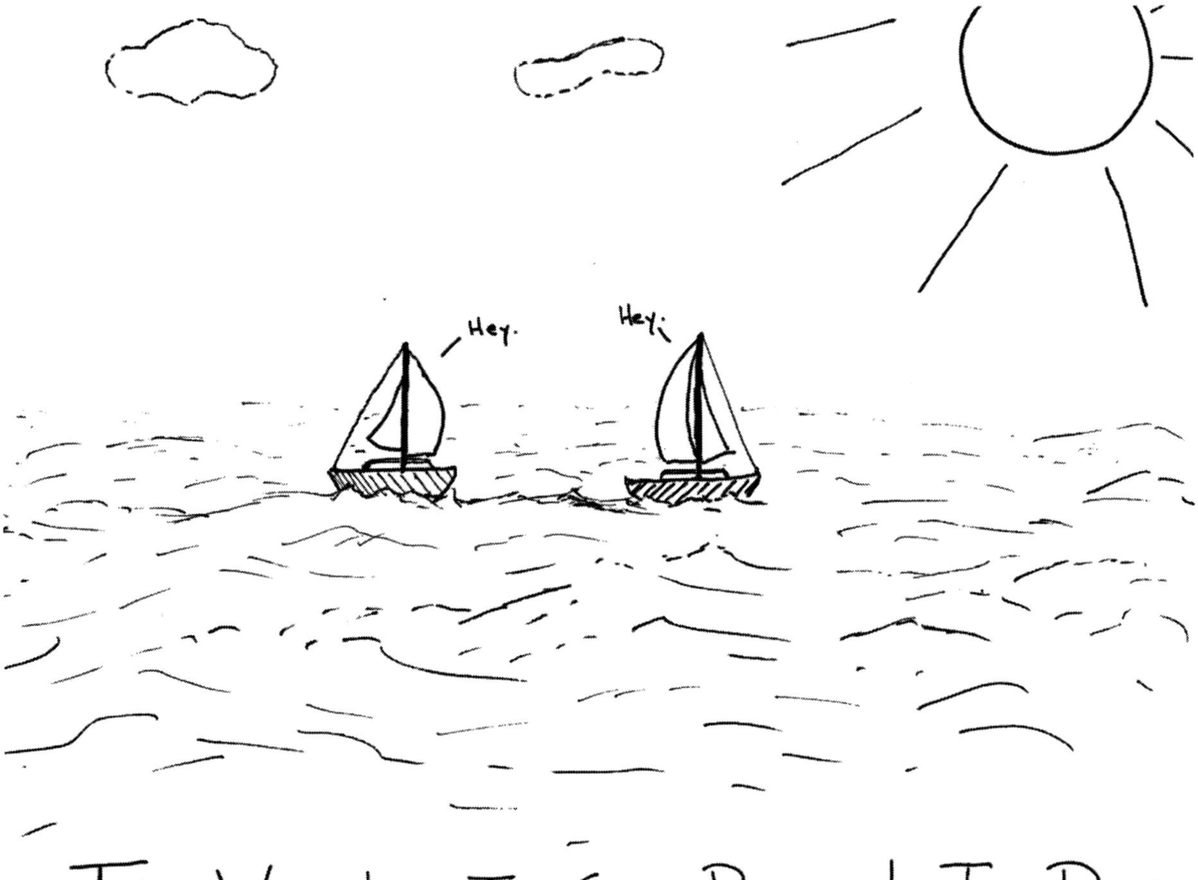
Hey.
Hey.

THEY WERE LIKE TWO SHIPS, PASSING IN THE DAY.

Little Known Fact: The Beanie Baby Boom of the Mid-90's can be Traced to Stricter Beanie Abortion Laws Passed in 1994.

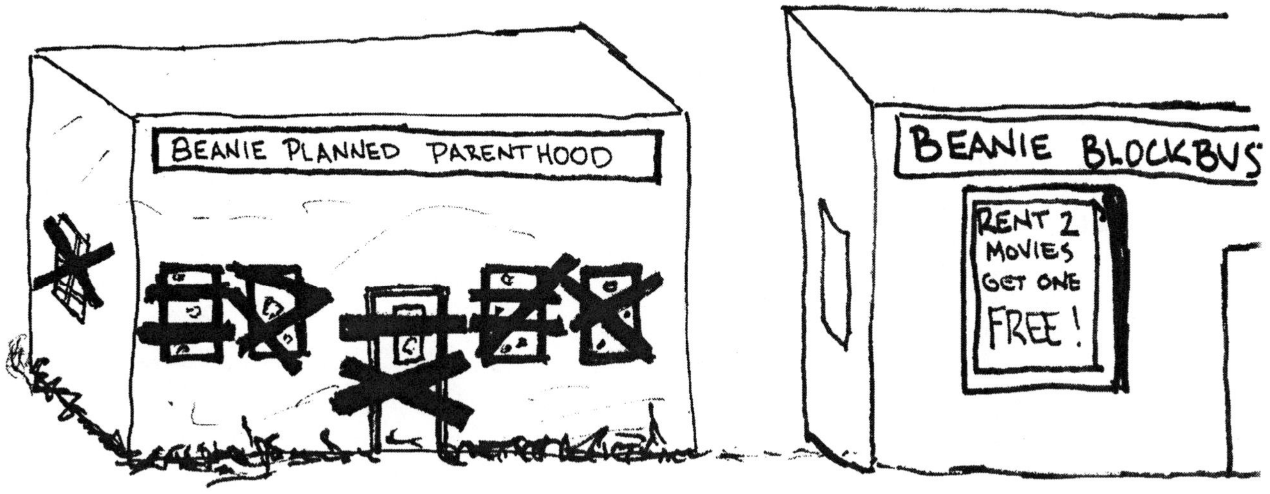
BEANIE PLANNED PARENTHOOD
BEANIE BLOCKBUS
RENT 2 MOVIES GET ONE FREE!

Taylor Lautner, please.
Call. I writhe, nightly, against
your body pillow.

· Beth Lautner

SAD HAIKU: TAYLOR

BILL THE BELLIGERENT BUNNY
VISITS THE RETIREMENT HOME

AM I YOUR GRANDSON?
WELL, LET ME ASK YOU A
QUESTION. DOES YOUR
GRANDSON SHIT PELLETS?
IF SO, THEN YES.

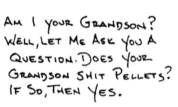

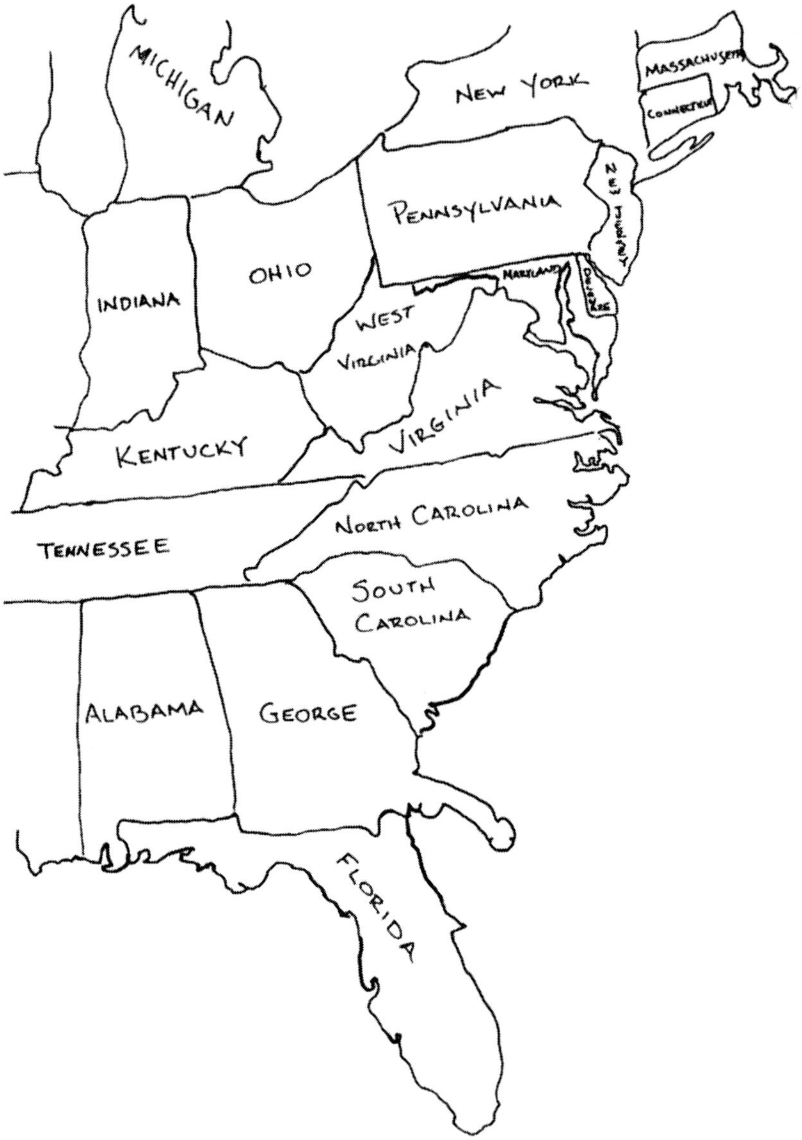
MICHIGAN
NEW YORK
PENNSYLVANIA
INDIANA
OHIO
WEST VIRGINIA
KENTUCKY
VIRGINIA
NORTH CAROLINA
TENNESSEE
SOUTH CAROLINA
ALABAMA
GEORGE
FLORIDA

East Coast Sex Change

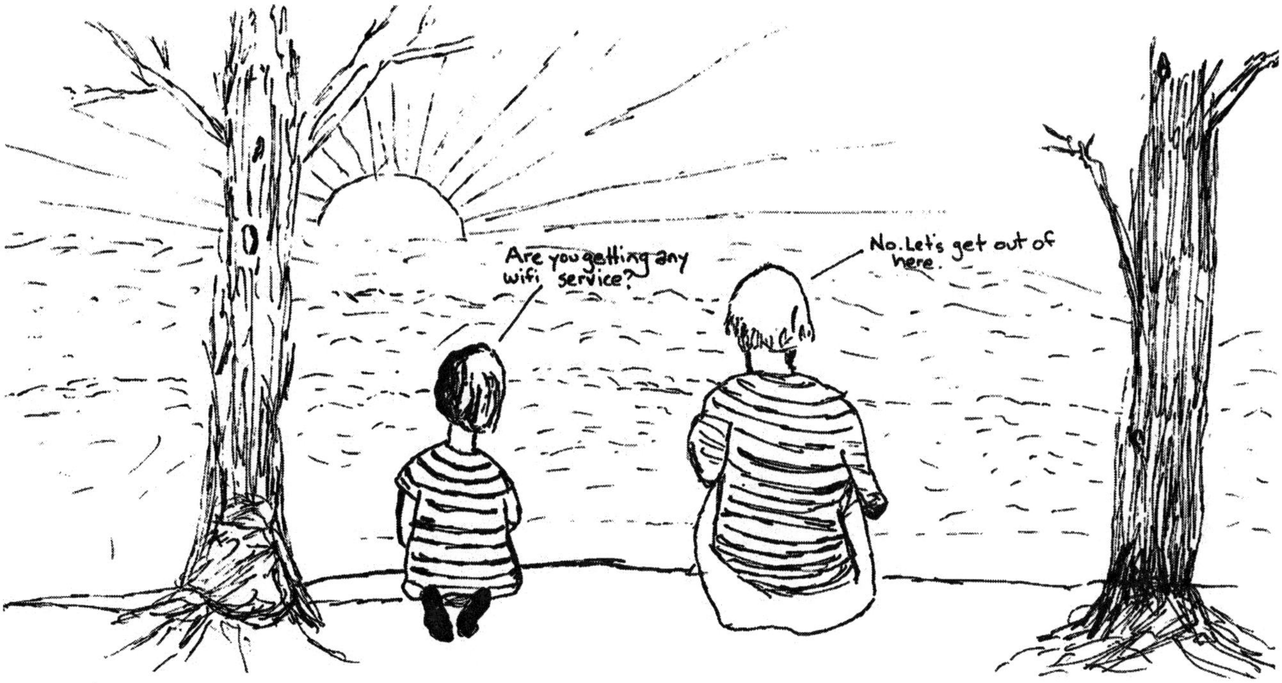
Are you getting any wifi service?
No. Let's get out of here.

She was worried. He always remembered to call.

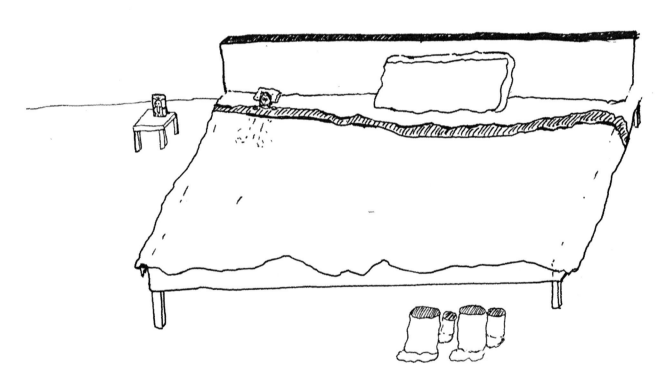

No St. Bart's this year.

Worse? My 6-year-old's birthday

is now sans Bieber.

– Michael

SAD HAIKU: WALL STREET

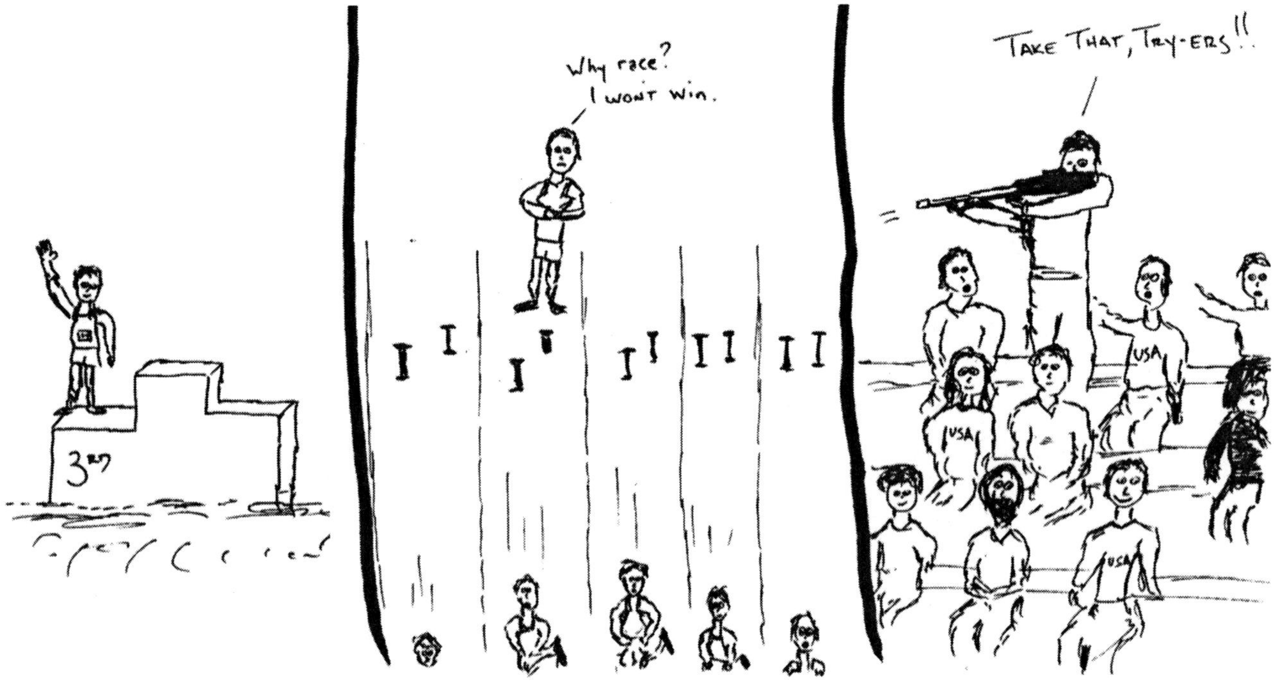
3RD
Why race? I wont win.
TAKE THAT, TRY-ERS!!
USA
USA
USA

A FOR EFFORT   C FOR EFFORT   F FOR EFFORT

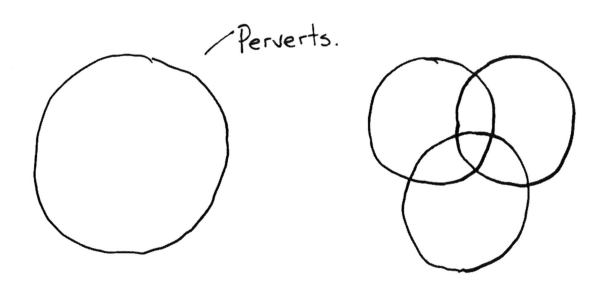

Perverts.

SPADER TOT

Exclusively on XM Radio

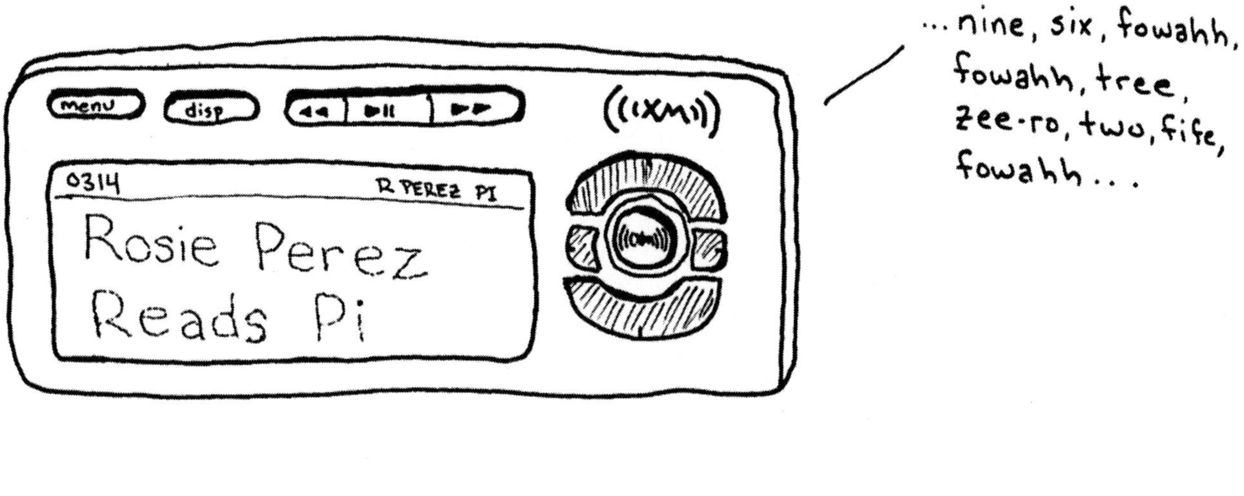
menu
disp
((XM))
0314
R PEREZ PI
Rosie Perez
Reads Pi
...nine, six, fowahh,
fowahh, tree,
zee-ro, two, fife,
fowahh...

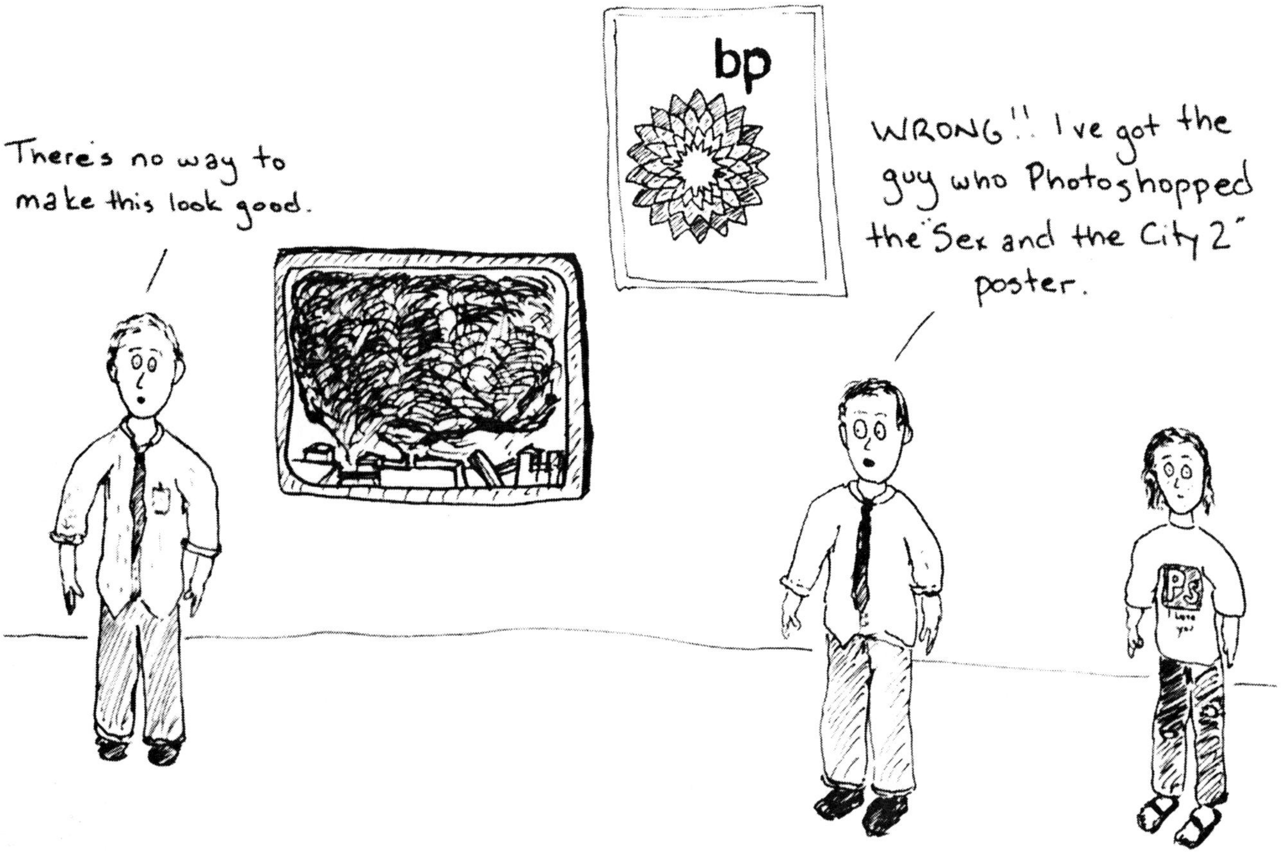
There's no way to make this look good.
bp
WRONG!! I've got the guy who Photoshopped the "Sex and the City 2" poster.
PS

THE BEGINNING OF THE WEEK WASN'T LOOKING GOOD.

SUNDAY	MONDAY	TUESDAY	WEDNESDAY	THURSDAY	FRIDAY	SATURDAY
SUNNY	DISAPPOINTED	BETRAYED	AFRAID OF YOU	GETTING OVER IT	SUNNY	SUNNY
72°	65°	61°	64°	66°	68°	71°

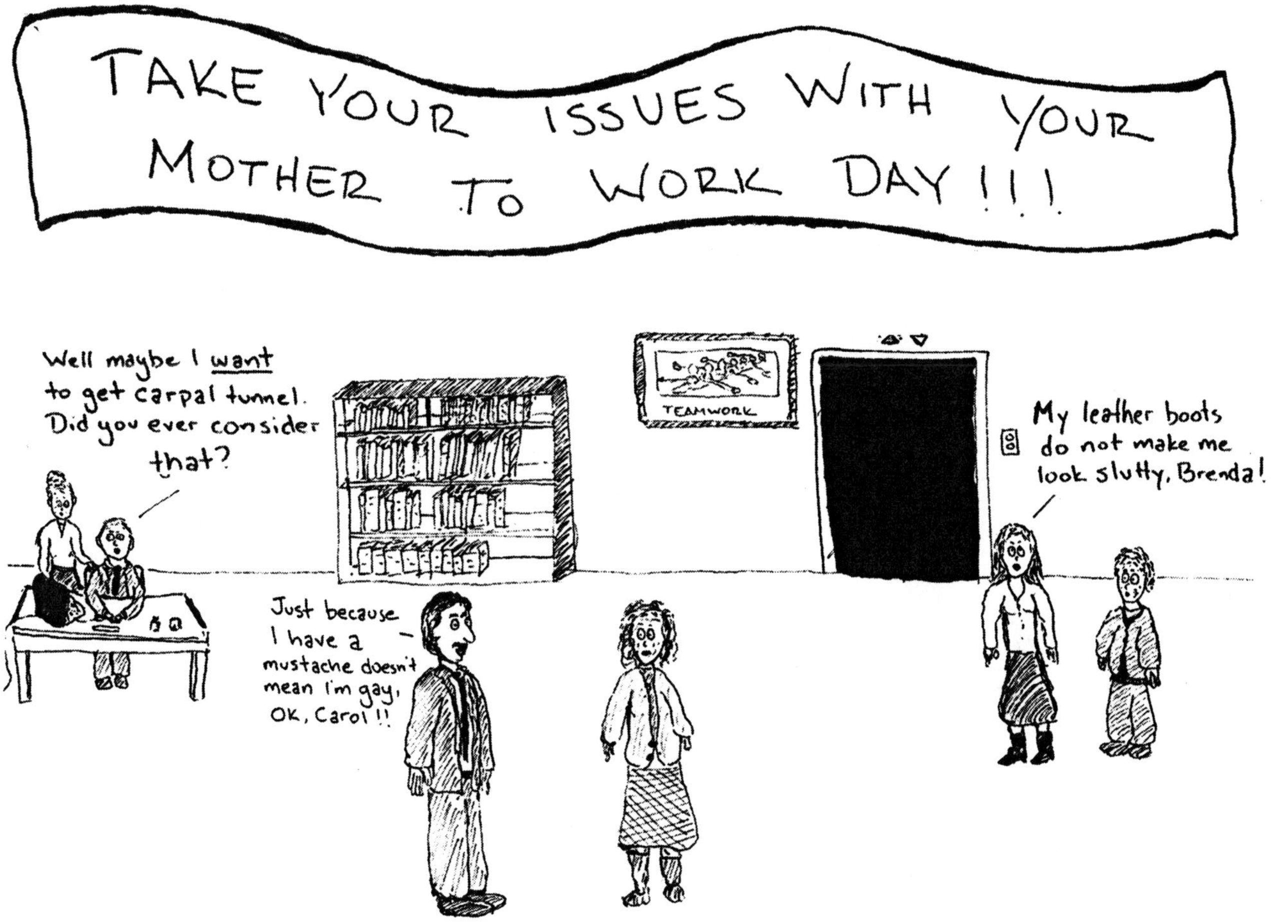
TAKE YOUR ISSUES WITH YOUR MOTHER TO WORK DAY!!!
Well maybe I want to get carpal tunnel. Did you ever consider that?
TEAMWORK
My leather boots do not make me look slutty, Brenda!
Just because I have a mustache doesn't mean I'm gay, OK, Carol!!

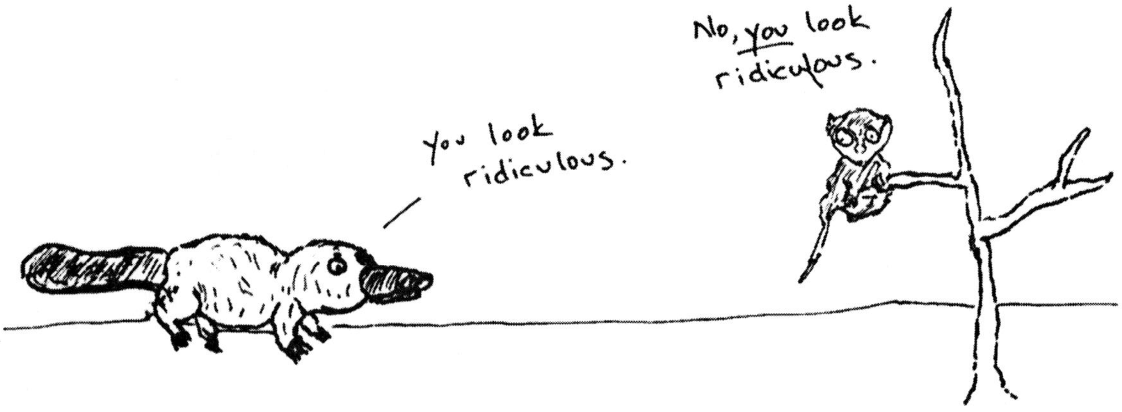
You look ridiculous.
No, you look ridiculous.

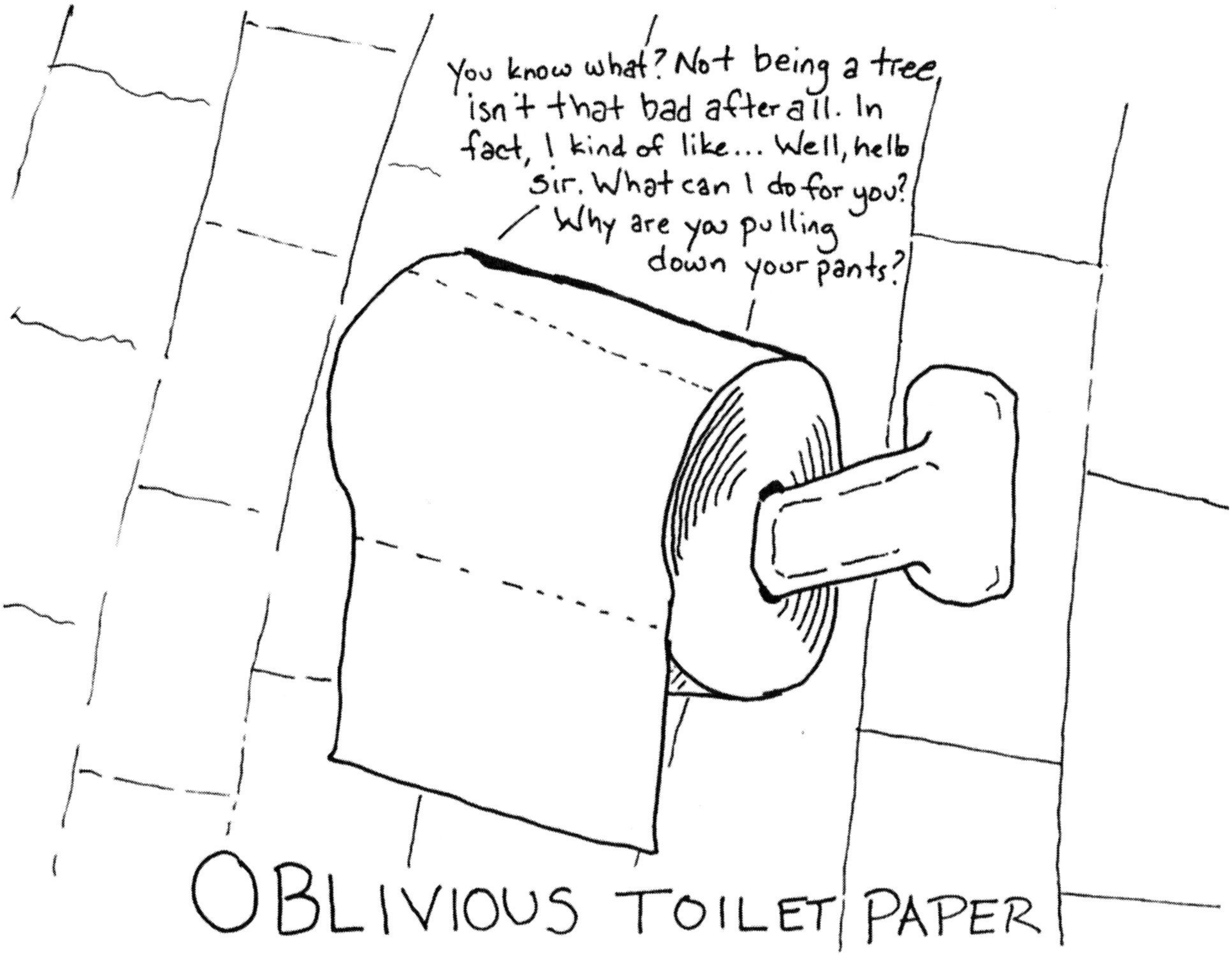
You know what? Not being a tree, isn't that bad after all. In fact, I kind of like... Well, hello sir. What can I do for you? Why are you pulling down your pants?
OBLIVIOUS TOILET PAPER

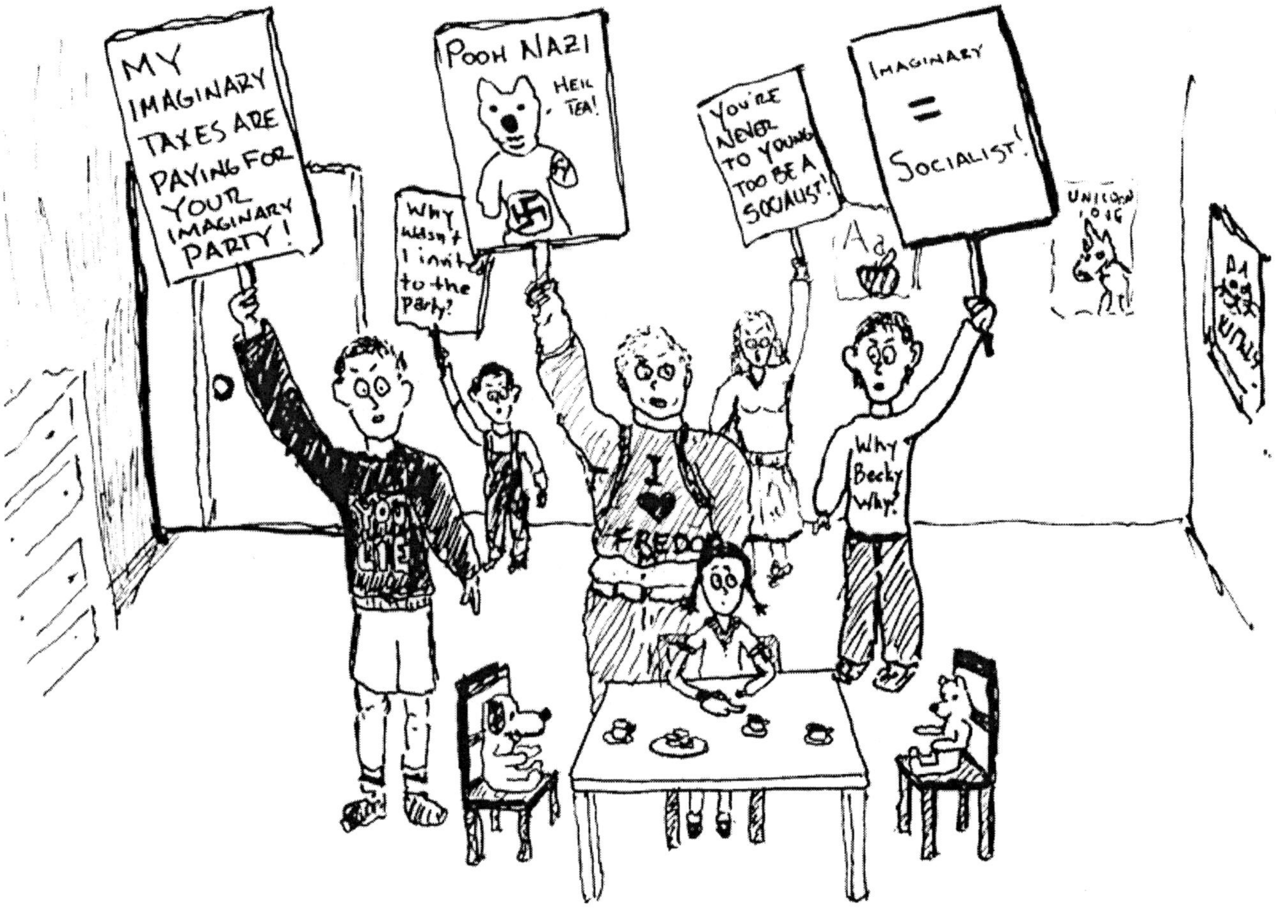
MY IMAGINARY TAXES ARE PAYING FOR YOUR IMAGINARY PARTY!
POOH NAZI
HEIL TEA!
Why wasn't I invit to the party?
YOU'RE NEVER TO YOUNG TOO BE A SOCIALIST!
IMAGINARY = SOCIALIST!
Why Becky Why?

TEA PARTY TEA PARTY

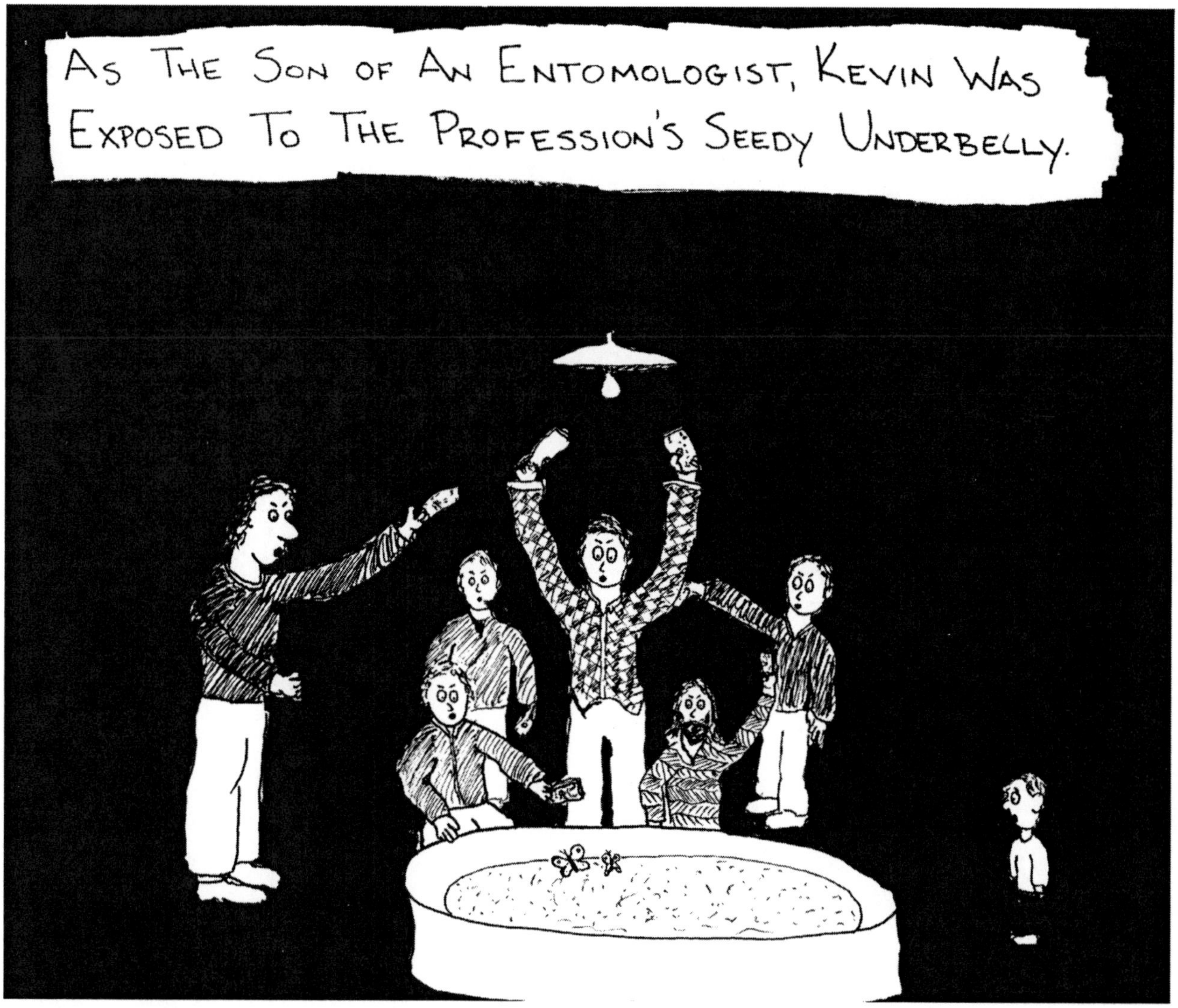
AS THE SON OF AN ENTOMOLOGIST, KEVIN WAS EXPOSED TO THE PROFESSION'S SEEDY UNDERBELLY.

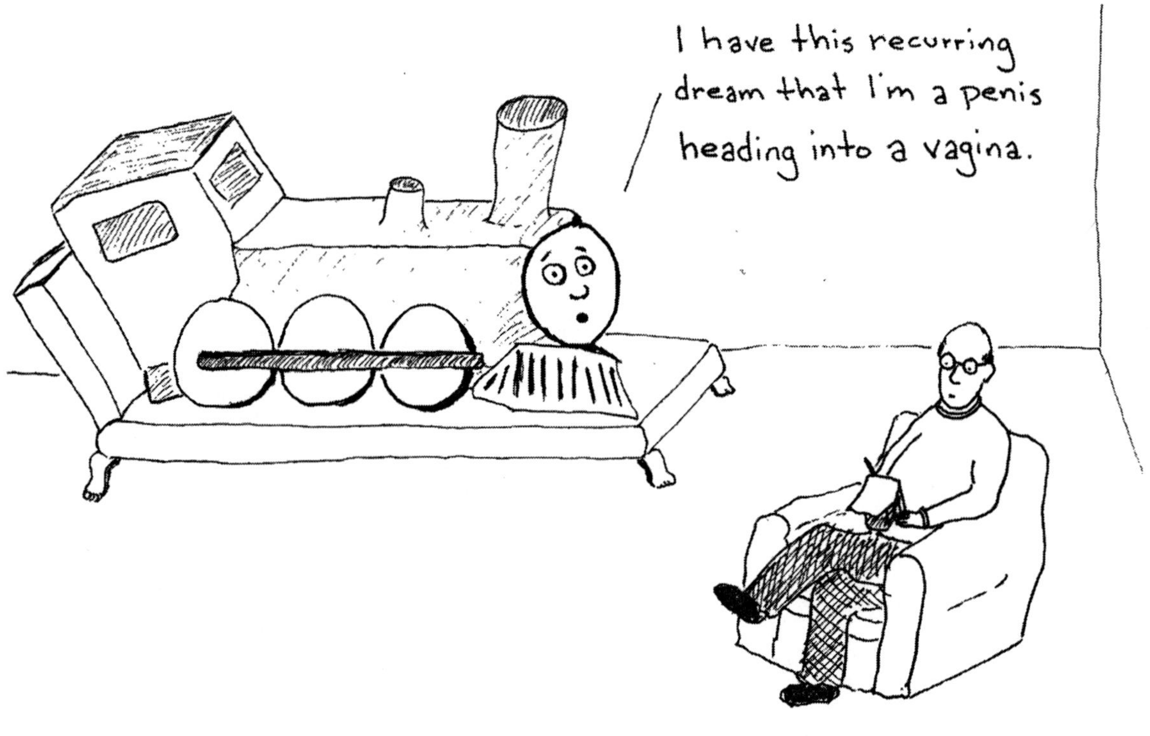
I have this recurring dream that I'm a penis heading into a vagina.

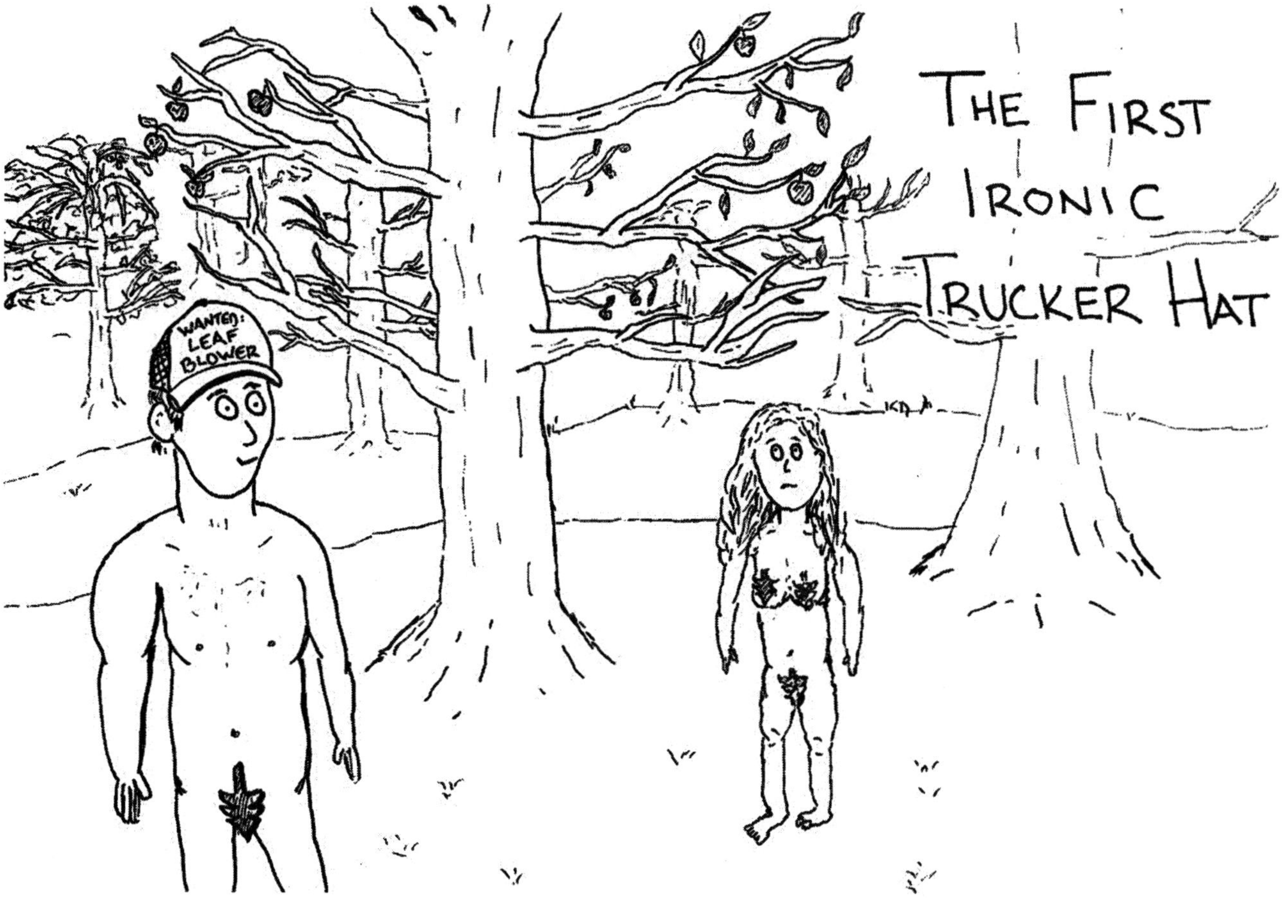
THE FIRST
IRONIC
TRUCKER HAT
WANTED:
LEAF
BLOWER

He was made of the alphabet,
which gave him insane Scrabble skills.

More Things Need Tusks

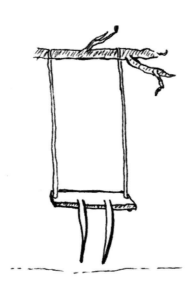

Tusk!

Sunflowers

Tree Swings

Stevie Nicks

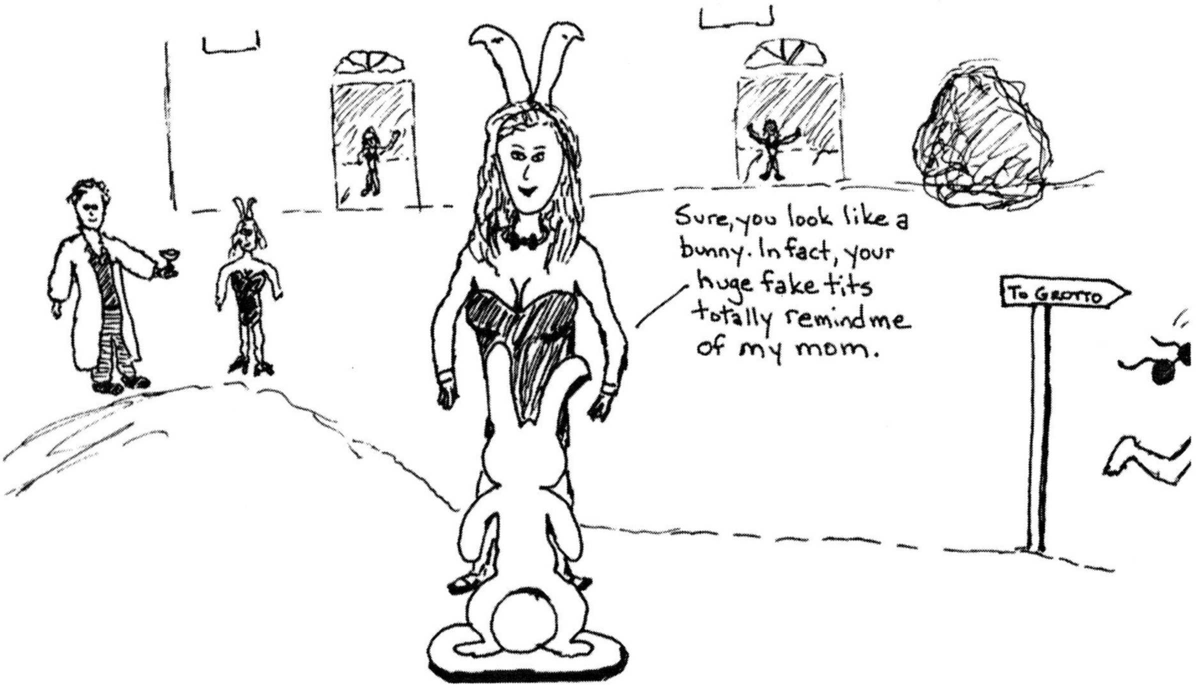
Sure, you look like a bunny. In fact, your huge fake tits totally remind me of my mom.
To Grotto

Bill The Belligerent Bunny
Visits The Playboy Mansion

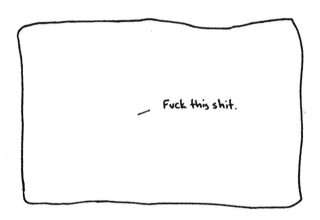

Somewhere in the middle of Wyoming,
he lost it completely.

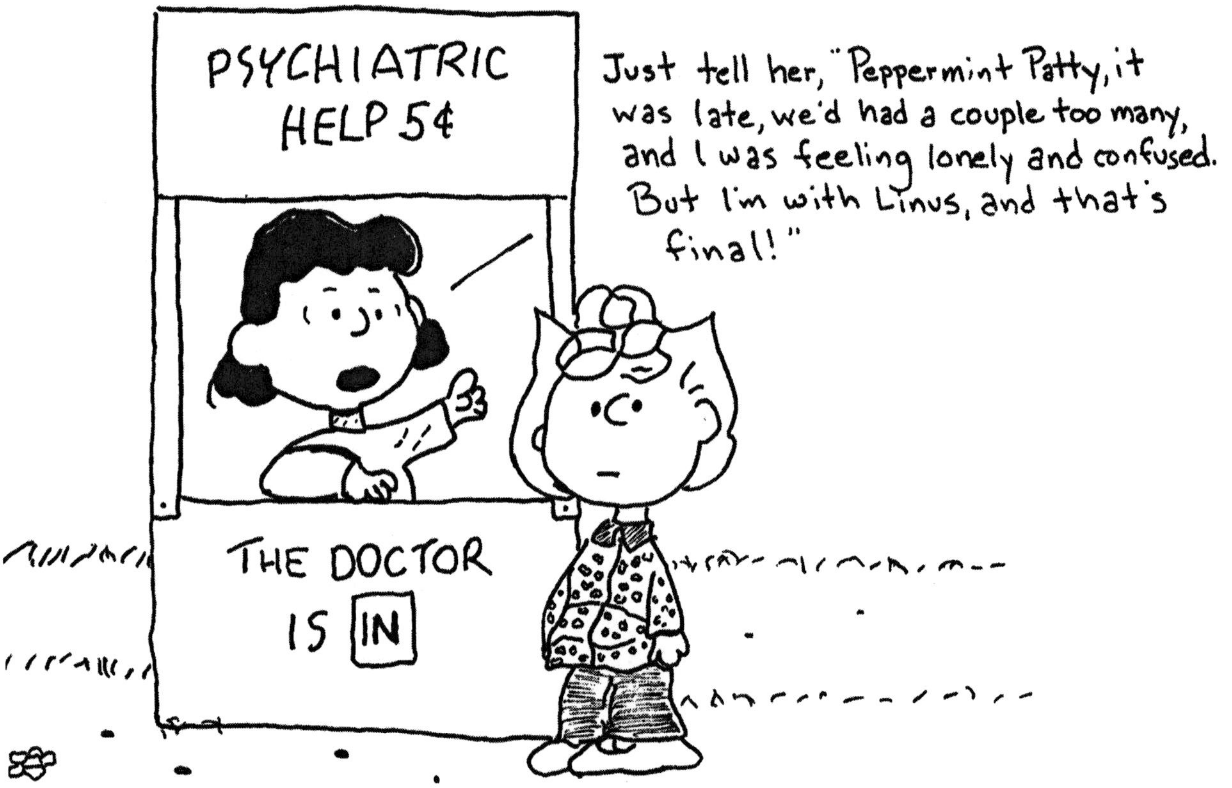
PSYCHIATRIC HELP 5¢
Just tell her, "Peppermint Patty, it was late, we'd had a couple too many, and I was feeling lonely and confused. But I'm with Linus, and that's final!"
THE DOCTOR IS IN

Dressing kids like adults isn't always cute.

THE POWER OUT, BOB TRIED TO SALVAGE THE BACHELOR PARTY

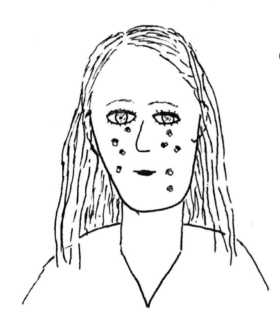

She was beautiful, intelligent, kind, and cried tiny chocolate cupcakes.

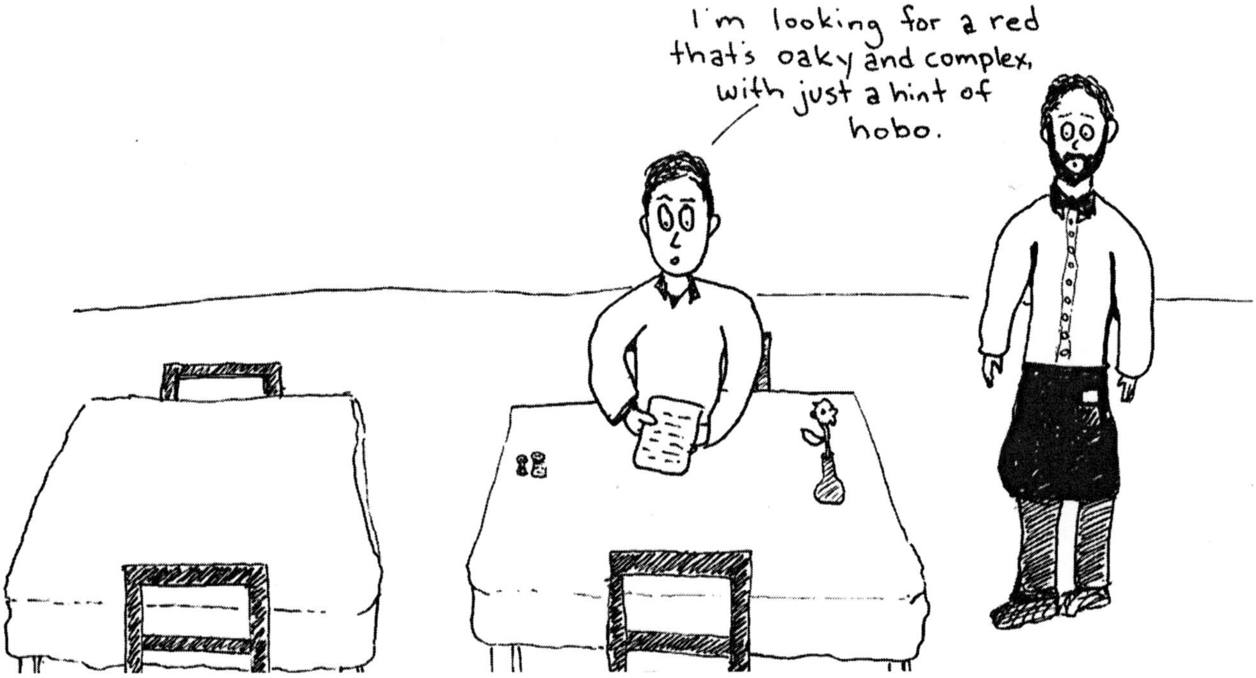
I'm looking for a red that's oaky and complex, with just a hint of hobo.

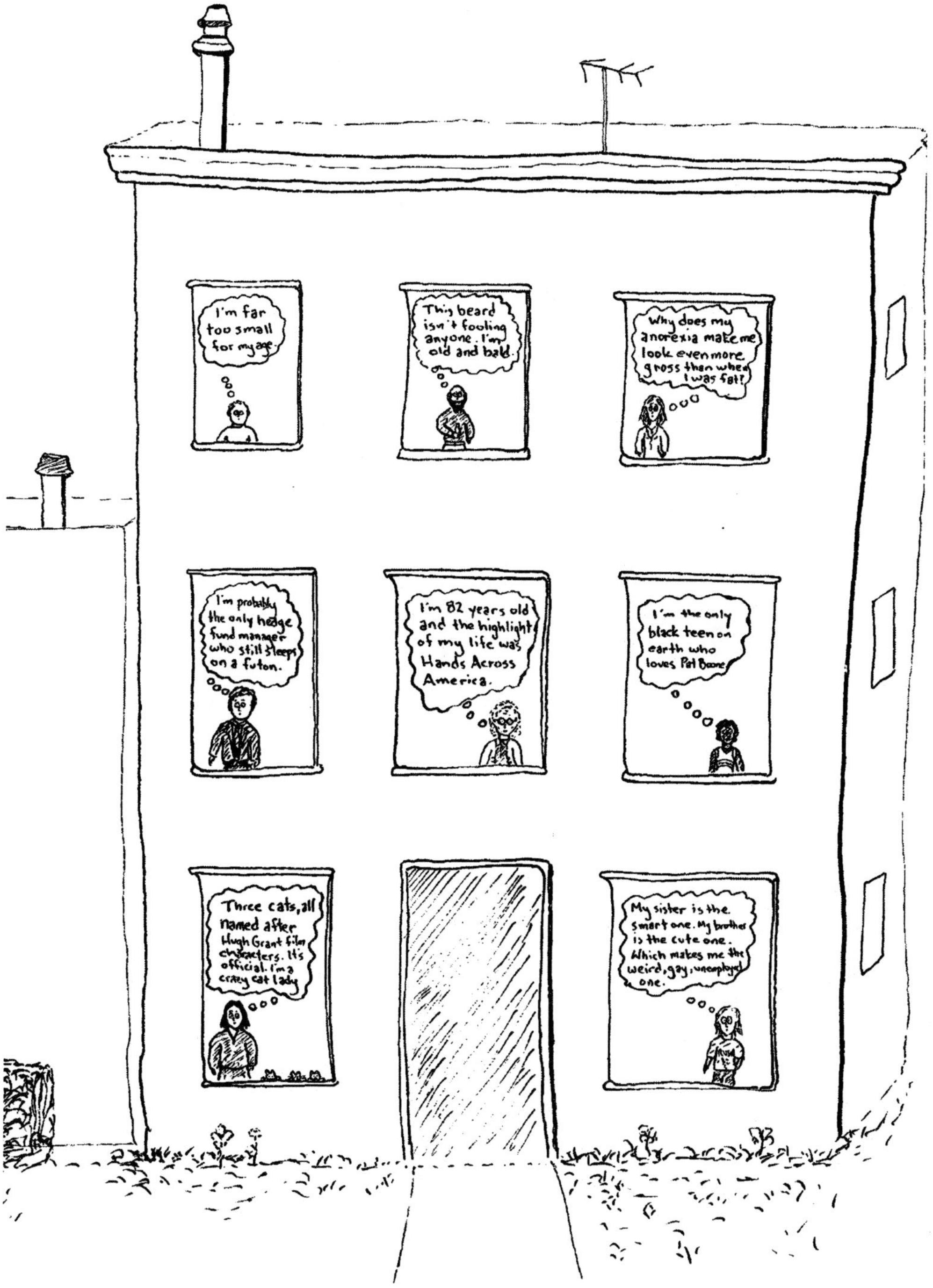
I'm far too small for my age.
This beard isn't fooling anyone. I'm old and bald.
Why does my anorexia make me look even more gross than when I was fat?
I'm probably the only hedge fund manager who still sleeps on a futon.
I'm 82 years old and the highlight of my life was Hands Across America.
I'm the only black teen on earth who loves Pat Boone.
Three cats, all named after Hugh Grant film characters. It's official. I'm a crazy cat lady
My sister is the smart one. My brother is the cute one. Which makes me the weird, gay, unemployed one.

THE INFERIORITY COMPLEX

If by "carrot" you mean four Manhattans, followed by an Old Fashioned, extra bitter, and three shots of Old Crow, then yes, bartender, I'd love a carrot.

BILL THE BELLIGERENT BUNNY
VISITS THE HOTEL BAR

OHIO, HAVING THE NAKED DREAM AGAIN

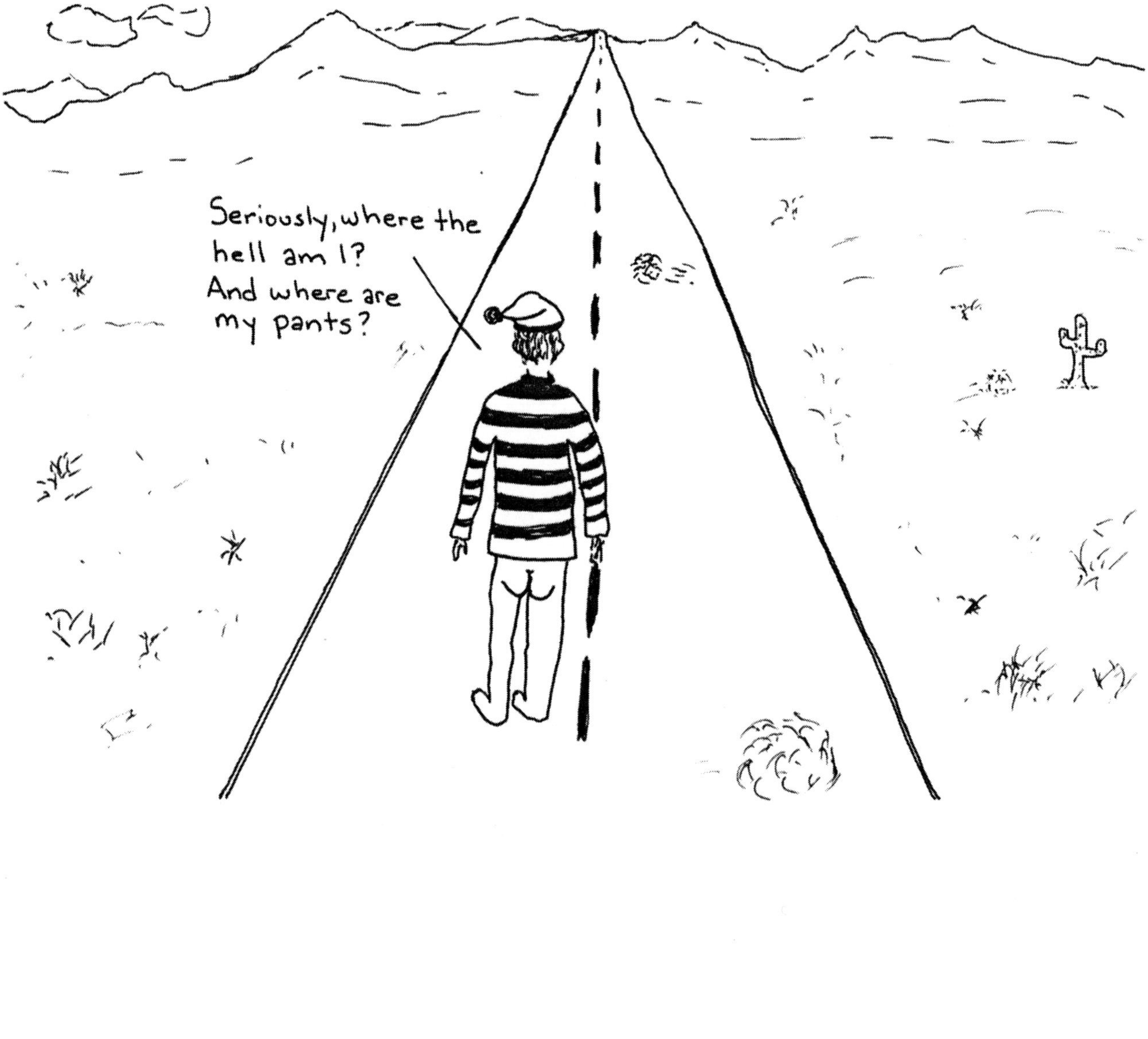
Seriously, where the hell am I? And where are my pants?

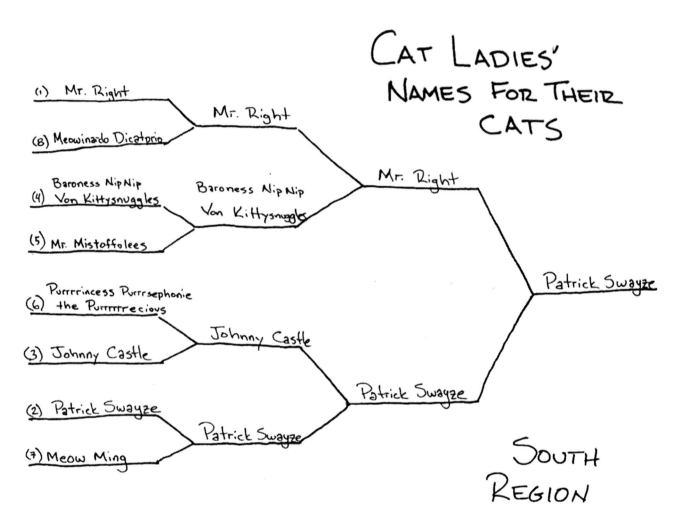

CAT LADIES' NAMES FOR THEIR CATS

(1) Mr. Right

Mr. Right

(8) Meowinardo Dicatprio

Mr. Right

Baroness Nip Nip
(4) Von Kittysnuggles

Baroness Nip Nip
Von Kittysnuggles

(5) Mr. Mistoffolees

Mr. Right

Purrrrincess Purrrsephonie
(6) the Purrrrrrecious

Johnny Castle

(3) Johnny Castle

Patrick Swayze

Patrick Swayze

(2) Patrick Swayze

Patrick Swayze

(7) Meow Ming

SOUTH REGION

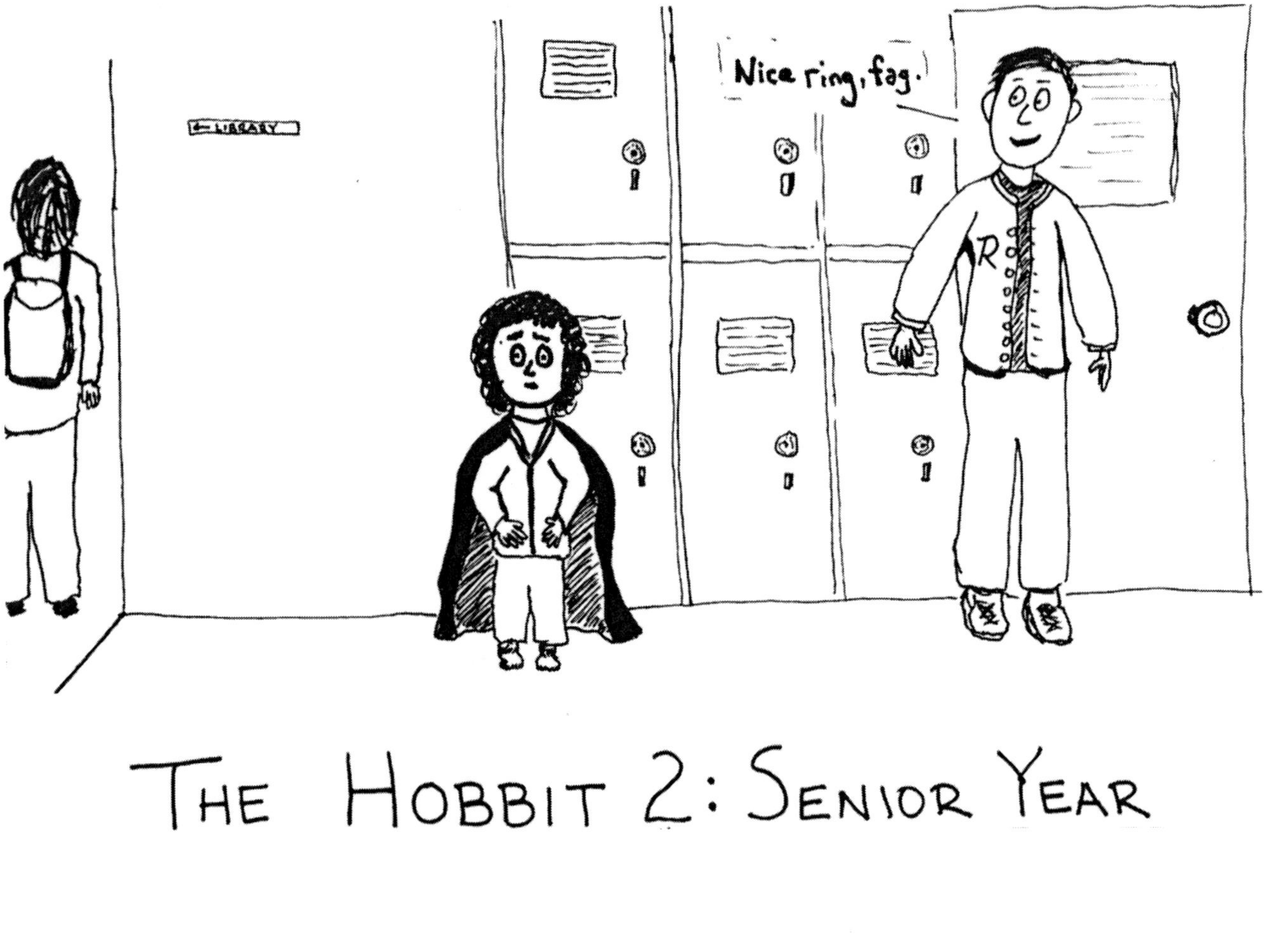
LIBRARY
Nice ring, fag.

THE HOBBIT 2: SENIOR YEAR

FAT TETRIS

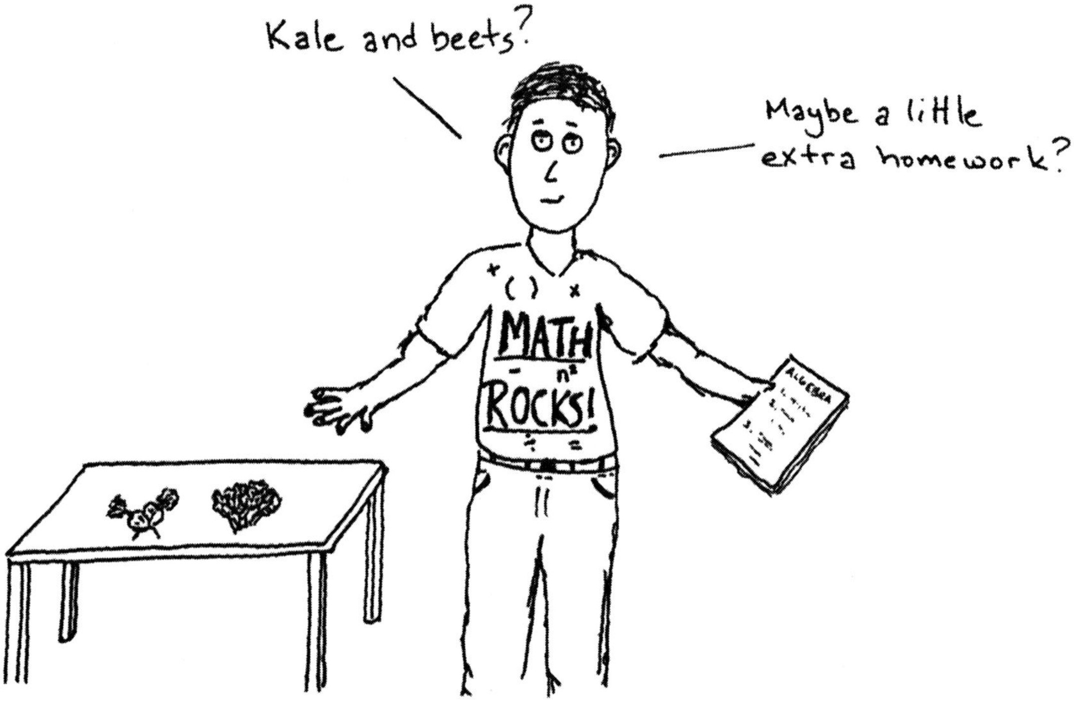
Kale and beets?
Maybe a little extra homework?
MATH
ROCKS!
ALGEBRA

World's Worst Sexual Predator

$$\text{GENIUS} =$$

1%	INSPIRATION
1%	NOTEWORTHY OUTFITS
8%	FOREIGN ACCENT
3%	FACIAL HAIR / PROMINENT MOLE
6%	UNSPOKEN CHILDHOOD TRAUMA
1%	WIENER / BOOB SIZE
.25%	EXOTIC PET OWNERSHIP
.25%	LACK OF INTEREST IN SPORTS
.5%	ASSOCIATION WITH BONO
10%	IN DEPTH KNOWLEDGE OF APPLE PRODUCTS
10%	ABILITY TO PULL OFF WEARING A HAT WITHOUT LOOKING LIKE AN ASS
43%	FRIENDSHIPS WITH PEOPLE ON THE BOARD OF THE MACARTHUR FELLOWSHIP
16%	PERSPIRATION

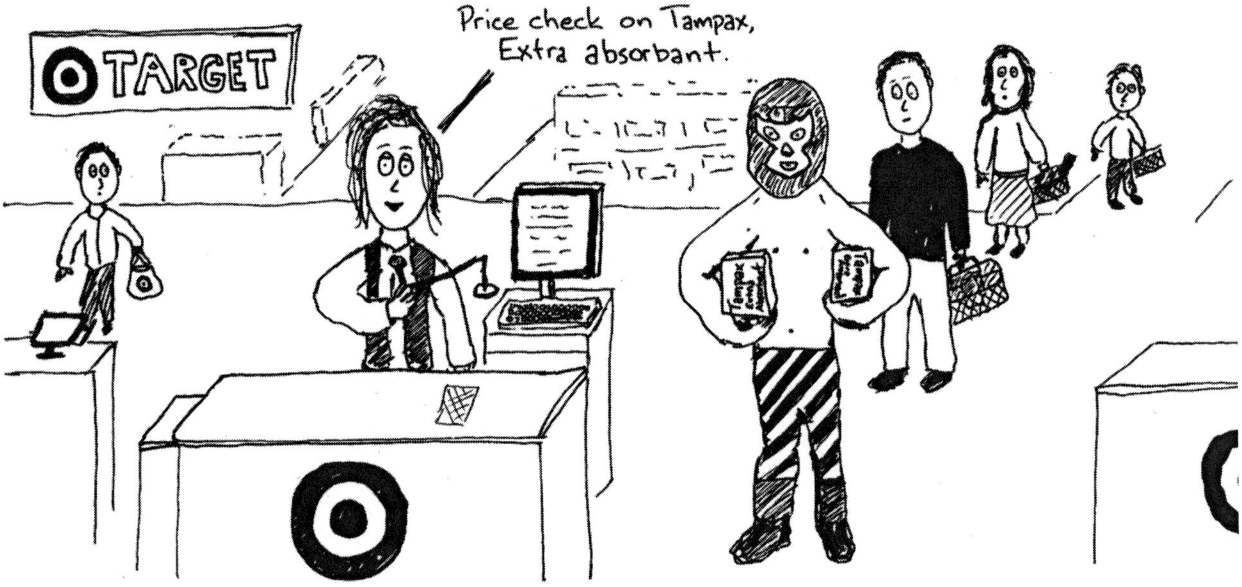
TARGET
Price check on Tampax,
Extra absorbant.

La Tormenta Gigante Suffers His First Crushing Defeat.

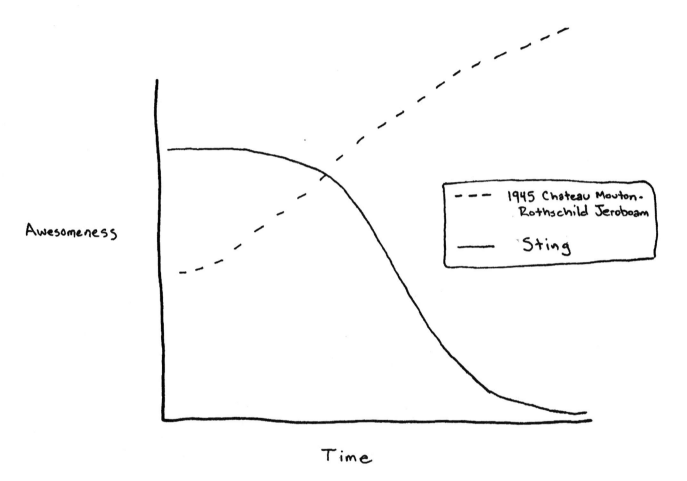

Awesomeness

Time

1945 Chateau Mouton-
Rothschild Jeroboam

Sting

UM, EXCUSE ME, SIR, BUT WHAT WOULD YOU CONSIDER "NATURE'S DONUT?"

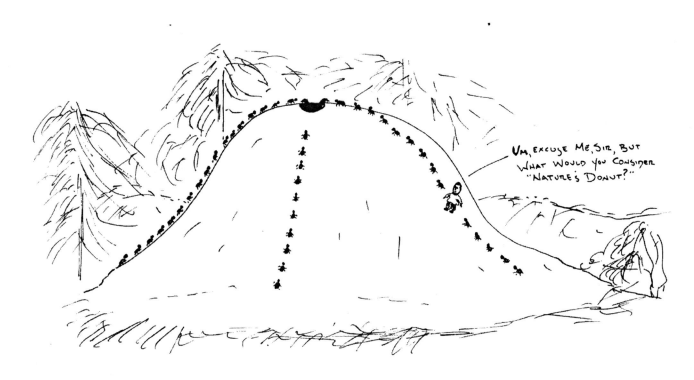

HONEY, I SHRUNK THE PUDGY KID

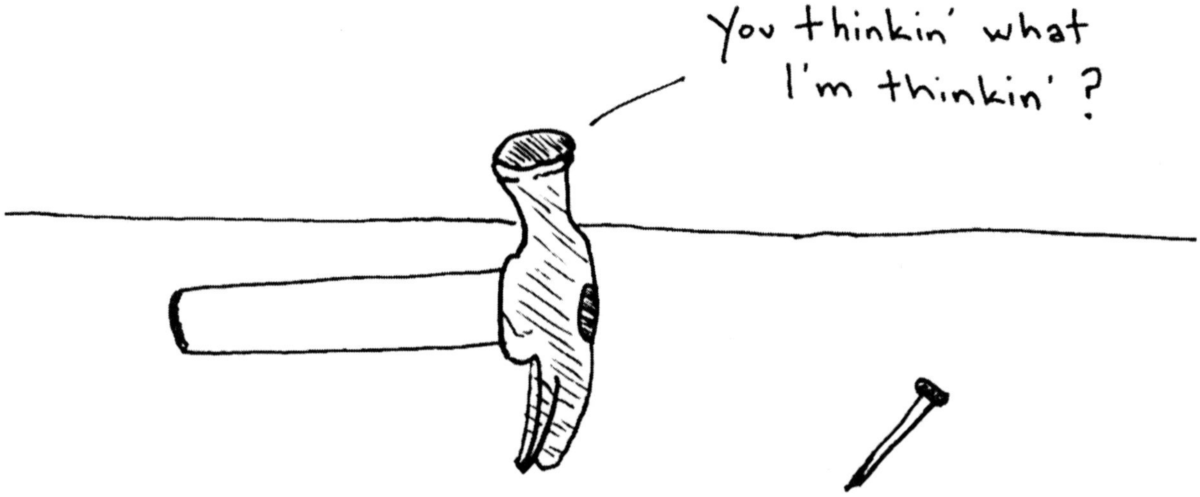
You thinkin' what I'm thinkin'?

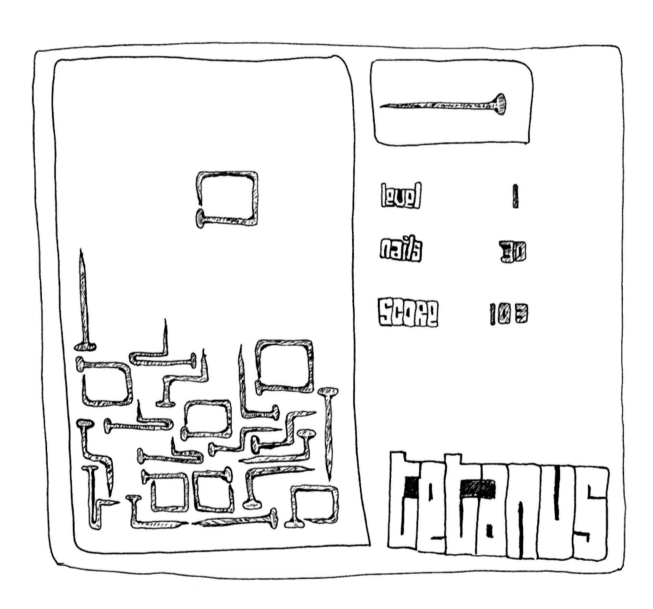

level   1

nails   30

score   103

tetanus

DOCTORS WITHOUT BORDERS

MOON JUMPING PRACTICE: DAY ONE

My mom called it "cute."

My grandparents laughed out loud.

Yep, my sex tape blows.

- Neal Y. -

SAD HAIKU : TAPE

Some day, I want to be famous enough to completely lose perspective.

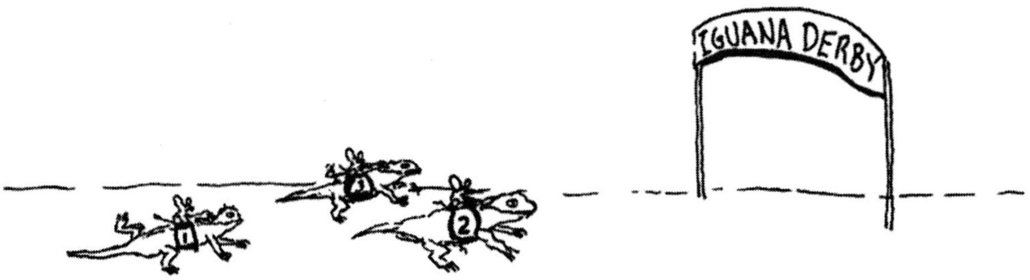
IGUANA DERBY
1
2

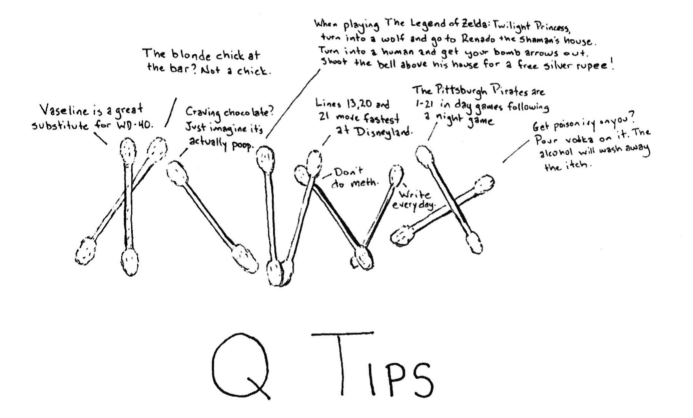

Vaseline is a great substitute for WD-40.

The blonde chick at the bar? Not a chick.

Craving chocolate? Just imagine it's actually poop.

When playing The Legend of Zelda: Twilight Princess, turn into a wolf and go to Renado the Shaman's house. Turn into a human and get your bomb arrows out. Shoot the bell above his house for a free silver rupee!

Lines 13,20 and 21 move fastest at Disneyland.

The Pittsburgh Pirates are 1-21 in day games following a night game.

Get poison ivy on you? Pour vodka on it. The alcohol will wash away the itch.

Don't do meth.

Write every day.

Q TIPS

I need a fuckin' drink.

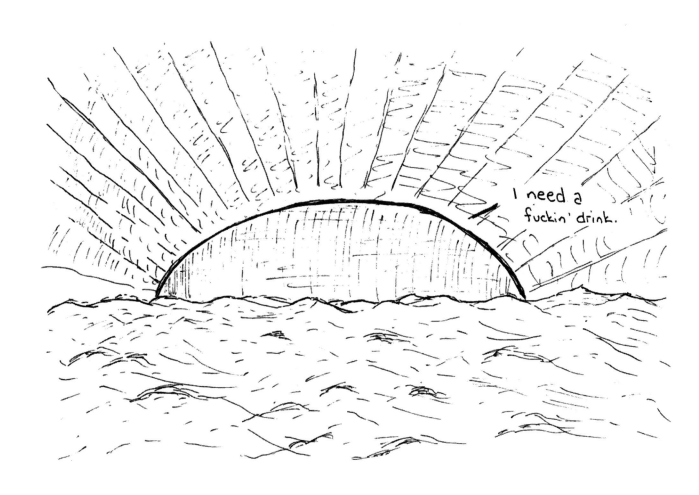

Index

TED McCAGG is not an artist by trade. In fact, he has spent the past fifteen years in the world of advertising as a writer. He did take a drawing class in college, but only because it was considered an easy A. He lives in San Francisco with his wife and daughter, but hopes to move to Portland sometime soon so he can afford a house.

Ted is available for idle chat/children's birthday parties at paperdollorgy@gmail.com.

LaVergne, TN USA
19 January 2011

213147LV00006B/1/P